WHY NOT WIN?

WHY NOT WIN?

Reflections on a Fifty-year Journey from the Segregated South to America's Boardrooms

— And What It Can Teach Us All

Larry D. Thornton

Foreword by Tom Joyner

NewSouth Books

Montgomery

NewSouth Books
105 S. Court Street
Montgomery, AL 36104

Library of Congress Cataloging-in-Publication Data

Names: Thornton, Larry D., author.
Title: Why not win? : reflections on a fifty-year journey from the segregated
  South to America's boardrooms and what it can teach us all / Larry D.
  Thornton ; foreword by Tom Joyner.
Description: Montgomery : NewSouth Books, [2019].
Identifiers: LCCN 2018055370 (print) | LCCN 2018059688 (ebook) | ISBN
  9781588383853 (Ebook) | ISBN 9781588383846 (hardcover)
Subjects: LCSH: Thornton, Larry D. | African American executives--Biography.
  | African American businesspeople--Biography. | Racism--United States. |
  Success--United States.
Classification: LCC HC102.5.T4595 (ebook) | LCC HC102.5.T4595 A3 2019
  (print) | DDC 338.092 [B] --dc23
LC record available at https://lccn.loc.gov/2018055370

Design by Randall Williams

Printed in the United States of America

To my children and grandchildren Catrina, Dale, Kadesha, Tre, and Paige for their daily examples and their quiet and subtle encouragement for my continued quest to "win" in life.

ACKNOWLEDGMENTS

I'd like to first say thank you to June Dunham, my former Coca-Cola colleague and the primary inspiration for both initiating and completing this literary project. Thanks as well to Marie Sutton, Jim Noles, and Zillah Fluker for your support with editing, content, structure, and historical relevance.

And then to my dear sister, and one of the most unassuming individuals that I know, Barbara Carter . . . for your consistent love and unwavering support of your brother.

And finally to far too many, named and unnamed, to mention for your deliberate and inadvertent support of my daily efforts to foster an attitude of "winning" for everyone around me . . . in each and every day of their lives.

CONTENTS

FOREWORD

TOM JOYNER

I find the parallels in mine and Larry Thornton's experiences in life very interesting. A constant theme of experience, exposure and commitment to education is interwoven through them. Larry and I were separated by less than forty miles during our childhoods and throughout our undergraduate studies—Larry attended Alabama State University and I attended Tuskegee University. Thinking about our proximity to one another has often made me wonder what it would be like to go back in time just to observe how often our paths crossed back then. More than likely we attended many of the same Turkey Day Classics. The rivalry between Tuskegee and ASU is one of many things of which Larry and I have fond memories (I must take this opportunity to highlight that my alma mater usually won!).

Larry is, by any and all definitions, a true Renaissance man. He epitomizes the impact that an alumnus of a Historically Black College or University (HBCU) has in his community. He possesses a rare combination of keen business acumen, accomplished artistry, and compassionate philanthropy. The best thing about Larry is that he gives not for public recognition or out of a sense of obligation. He gives because he cares about the people he helps. Moreover, Larry gives to the causes he is involved with the more precious gift of his time.

My late brother, Al Joyner, was an established McDonald's owner/operator in Alabama. Amongst other things, Larry is also a McDonald's owner/operator. The irony here is that when Larry was training to become an owner/operator, he actually trained under the tutelage of my brother at one of his Jefferson County stores. That seems most appropriate for another "Skegee alum" to teach a lesson or two to a "Bama State alum"!

I have been a long-time partner with McDonald's and Coca-Cola. Both are global, socially responsible brands. As an advocate of HBCUs, I have spent many Halloween weekends at what has become the nation's best-attended HBCU gathering, the annual Magic City Classic match-up in Birmingham between Alabama State University and Alabama A&M University. I appreciated during the Classic's seventy-fifth anniversary that Larry worked tirelessly with each school and the Bruno Event Team to secure major sponsorship dollars to establish the "McDonald's Magic City Classic presented by Coca-Cola."

Why Not Win? is another premier example of Larry giving back. He has taken the time to articulate the details of his life and showcase how his experiences shaped him into the person he is today. This book is a masterful life lesson for all ages. It makes me proud that a fellow HBCU alumnus has taken the time to do this.

Larry and I understand the importance of education and educating through life lessons. The late Nelson Mandela said, "Education is the most powerful weapon which you can use to change the world." I hope I am not embarrassing Larry by sharing this, but similar to the Tom Joyner Foundation's focus on scholarships for HBCU students, Larry has made significant contributions to academic scholarships. Such a commitment supports the development of some of the most brilliant minds in the country.

It is an enormous pleasure and I am honored to have the opportunity to be a part of this book.

P.S. Go Golden Tigers!

Tom Joyner is an American radio host, host of the nationally syndicated Tom Joyner Morning Show, *and also founder of Reach Media Inc., the Tom Joyner Foundation, and BlackAmericaWeb.com. Tom is a Tuskegee, Alabama, native and a major advocate for historically black colleges and universities (HBCUs).*

INTRODUCTION

Zillah Fluker

One of the points of inspiration that I have in my home is a painting that portrays the simple gaze of a girl named Kenya who appears in a piece of art titled *Blue Halo*.

I find great solace in this piece of art that shows this young girl gazing from the canvas with a distinct, natural, innocent beauty that to me symbolizes the motherland of Africa, as Kenya opens her eyes to the distant horizons of a world she wishes to better understand. This piece of art also symbolizes my introduction to a fellow Alabama State University alum, Birmingham's Larry Thornton. After purchasing this art and doing a little research, I realized that I was in great company—among others who owned Larry's artwork were entertainment mogul Oprah Winfrey, former Secretary of State Dr. Condoleezza Rice, and even the former CEO of McDonald's Corporation, Don Thompson.

As I gazed at my newly acquired painting, I felt a yearning to better understand the motivation of Kenya's creator and artist. Hence, I introduced myself and made contact with Larry Thornton, artist and successful business entrepreneur.

During this time, I was the newly appointed chief development officer at our joint alma mater, and as such I wanted to understand both the soul of the artist as well as seize the opportunity to develop a relationship with such a successful alumnus who might help me meet other alumni and Alabama business leaders for the benefit of our university. Having been away from Alabama while living on the east coast of the U.S. for well over a decade, I needed a mentor like Larry to help me re-thread the fabric of my contacts within the Deep South and the Hornet Nation.

From my first contact with Larry, a deep and abiding friendship and business relationship was formed, which would subsequently grow into my cultivating him to give the largest planned gift in ASU's history at the time. Because of his leadership and largess, he quickly climbed the ASU ladder of success and became appointed by the governor and confirmed by the state senate as a member of the ASU Board of Trustees. He subsequently became its chairman; during his tenure, Larry made history for the university, as he played a part in the recruitment and hiring of ASU's first female president.

Making history, breaking barriers, and building bridges are constant themes in Larry's life. As a natural artist, he is reflective on the distance from his humble beginnings—born into the epicenter of Jim Crow segregation in Montgomery, Alabama—to the success he has achieved in life and business.

As a schoolboy, he was on the front lines of the fight to desegregate Montgomery's public schools. In 1979, one of his first adult jobs was as a sign painter for the local bottling company, Coca-Cola United, earning a whopping $5 an hour. Twenty years later, he would become the first and only African American to serve on the company's board of directors.

In 1994, he was the first African American named to the board of directors of Birmingham's highly respected First Commercial Bank (now Synovus). He also was the first African American to own a McDonald's franchise in the City of Birmingham—an entrepreneurial success that grew to six restaurants and that led to his election to the food giant's international board of directors and his service on the auditing committee of the McDonald's Owner/Operator Insurance Co. (MOOIC).

As often the only African American in his various business endeavors, Larry's road to success was filled with the landmines and potholes of racial struggle. He overcame and succeeded despite the adverse circumstances of prejudice, and from his experiences, he pulled key lessons that helped him achieve a great deal on his life's journey. He has always been generous in sharing these lessons, especially with young people.

I had heard parts of the Larry Thornton story over the years and in some instances had shared his lessons with my students as a motivational tool. Once, Larry and I, with the support of Coca-Cola United, collaborated on a leadership development student dinner. At the time, Larry was serving as the first and only African American member of the board of governors of the prestigious The Club, an exclusive dining club in Birmingham; in 2015, Larry was elected its first African American president. The Club served as a perfect location to host this student leadership dinner.

This book is an extension of Larry's sharing of his principles for living one's life. It is great to have a contextualized consolidation of these lessons to share with a broader population of people. These invaluable lessons can inspire all of us, regardless of race, gender or age, because the constant theme of Larry's life is about overcoming adversity and winning life's battles.

For a four-year period, I was at the helm of the Magic City Classic, the annual slugfest football game between Montgomery's Alabama State University and Huntsville's Alabama A&M University, which is played in Birmingham's historic Legion Field as a neutral site. Over the years, this matchup has grown into the largest spectacle and best-attended event among the nation's HBCUs. In my first year as the lead for one of the rival schools, I came to learn the significance of this event when the renowned radio personality, Tom Joyner, selected ASU as the October 2014 school of the month. This was an aggressive fundraising strategy because the Tom Joyner Morning Show was a major component of this more than 150,000-person gathering. Then, in 2016 on the occasion of the the Seventy-Fifth Magic City Classic, we renamed it as the "McDonald's Magic City Classic presented by Coca-Cola." Larry played a major role in bringing the City of Birmingham, the leadership of both universities, and the Bruno Event Team together to take full advantage of the two major global brands coming together to be a part of this historic event.

Now, the largest HBCU Classic in the nation would be headlined by two of the most recognized trademarks in the world—and Larry was the catalyst for this moment. As he took the microphone at the press conference, he confessed that he felt like he was "the luckiest guy in Birmingham." At the same time, however, onlookers who knew Larry understood that the moment was not just about McDonald's and Coca-Cola coming together on the HBCU stage. It was also a testament to his own gifts—his ability to "focus on relationships and leverage them for the greater good." No wonder his sense of joy and pride was so clearly visible to all of us around him.

In our brief time on earth, we encounter many people who shape our lives, directly and indirectly. Larry Thornton is one of those for me, particularly as it relates to my professional "brand" and how I choose to carry myself amongst my peers.

As a child of Africa and a product of an American education, I am conscious of the requirement to deliver above and beyond the minimum expectations, which Larry Thornton's life has shown me to be true. The greatest influence—one that readers will glean from this book—is the importance and value of good and positive relationships.

Returning to the beautiful Kenya, who remains eternally young in the painting displayed in my home, it is important that I mention her most unique feature—her eyes. They are hazel-brown and almost glow as if she is making direct eye contact with anyone who gazes on her countenance. Hers is an expression that instills a great sense of hope, innocence, and optimism.

Larry Thornton the artist gave her that expression. As you better understand Larry and his life's experiences through this book, you, too, will take away Kenya's sense of hope.

What you will learn is that despite the many challenges, roadblocks, adversities, and disadvantages in your personal path, if you—like Kenya and her creator—face the world with a sense of optimism, hope, discipline, and the right attitude, you, too, may ask the question, *Why Not Win?*

Zillah Fluker has been mentored by the author since 2012, shortly after purchasing Larry Thornton's Blue Halo *print. She is a seventeen-year leader in corporate America and higher education and is currently a social media engagement strategist, PhD candidate, and founder and principal for Activate\Elevate, LLC, a social media and marketing firm. She is a graduate of Alabama State University (ASU) and Purdue University, and served as ASU's Vice President of Institutional Advancement while Larry Thornton was chairman of the ASU Board of Trustees.*

Blue Halo
"When Kenya Meets the World"

PROLOGUE

For most of my life, I thought Jim Crow was a larger-than-life man, equivalent to the king of some far-off country or even the president of our own United States. Only such a giant could possess the strength and stature to oppress an entire race of people with dark skin like mine. Only such a titan could somehow validate a poisonous mindset amongst a group of people whose skin had a different tone than mine.

For decades, Mr. Jim's perpetual hate, with its far-reaching tentacles, extended its influential grip across the entire South—and even beyond. He even had an army of frightful followers—the hooded Ku Klux Klan and its fellow travelers—who enforced the laws and customs of the land in total submission to his insidious influence.

Growing up in Montgomery, Alabama, during the 1950s and '60s, I regularly witnessed the power of Mr. Jim's malicious presence. Blacks were relegated to subservient roles. They were barred from certain businesses and referred to by derogatory names, one of which would reduce an entire race of people to less than the dust beneath a shoe. It was as if Mr. Jim wanted to cast a shadow upon their very legitimacy. For whatever devilish reasons that propelled him, he had a venomous desire to denigrate and decimate even the smallest hint of their human existence.

At a very young age, I heard stories of Mr. Jim's cruel handiwork that cut to my core. In the wake of the Montgomery Bus Boycott, Rosa

Jordan, a pregnant black woman twenty-two years old, was shot by a sniper while she was sitting on a desegregated bus; this was on December 28, 1956, just a week after the jubilant conclusion of the year-long protest that ended segregated municipal bus seating. Barely a month later, Willie Edwards Jr., a black Winn-Dixie truck driver, was abducted by the KKK and forced to jump to his death off a high bridge into the murky Alabama River. For no other reason than hair texture and skin pigment, people with dark skin were often the subject of Jim Crow's wrath: intimidation, humiliation, threats, and worse, including beatings, disfigurements, and lynchings. And, according to Mr. Jim, it was all justifiable, a natural order of the times, and necessary to maintain the Southern "way of life."

As the years went by, I wondered about Mr. Jim's family—the Crows. I was curious if they had remained in the South and if they had any remorse or perhaps even repented for their sordid legacy. In fact, it wasn't until much later—and well into my professional career—that I realized Jim Crow was not a real person. I was sitting in a Birmingham restaurant, having a conversation with a friend, when she enlightened me. Her words pierced my soul. The reality of it all, for a moment, left me speechless.

Jim Crow, she explained, was, in truth, just a character dreamed up by an entertainer and then later used by a group of people to be the face of their dirty deeds. "Jim Crow" was created in the 1830s by Thomas Dartmouth Rice, a white minstrel performer born in New York City who would wear blackface makeup and sing and dance in an exaggerated manner he thought characterized that of enslaved black folks. The name "Jim Crow" came from the song "Jump, Jim Crow," to which Rice set his antics. Eventually, "Jim Crow" evolved into a derogatory term for African Americans and then became the name for the laws fashioned to keep blacks in their proverbial place.

No, Jim Crow did not have a family, a middle name, or even a pulse.

And, thinking back over my Southern childhood and young adulthood, I felt cheated by the deception. I had almost allowed this concept of a nonexistent man to snuff out my destiny—just as he had done to countless others.

Growing up under the omnipresent thumb of the phantom Jim Crow, I was socially and internally maladjusted. I was often angry—enraged even—because, for every single day, essentially everything around me reminded me that I was inferior for no other reason than being born. It was beat into me, spat at me, and posted on signs around me until it sank into my soul. It was stitched into my thinking like the worn patches that made up my grandmother's quilts. For that reason, I rejected school and disregarded and discounted people with white skin. It was a dangerous road I was on, and I was headed along it full-throttle.

Over time, however, something changed. Thanks to the help of caring people around me and a series of life lessons, I slowly but surely came to a seminal moment of clarity. At that moment, I saw myself not through the eyes of Jim Crow, but with eyes that recognized my value as a human being. I recognized and accepted that I had been endowed with an inherent ability to fashion my own thinking, free of the malign influence of Jim Crow and his "separate but (un)equal" progeny. I began to shake off thoughts of anger and inferiority and readied myself to approach life with a newly cleaned slate.

Although I knew it would not be easy to pursue a higher plane while living in the cradle of the segregated South, I would rely on endurance. If I can't take anything, I told myself, then I can't have anything. The more I could endure with grace and humility, the more I could have—no matter what Jim Crow or his disciples thought.

Today, I know that my change in thinking rewrote my history. Since then, I have been immensely fortunate and blessed with a wealth of opportunities—beyond my imagination and more than I deserve.

Today, I believe that people, situations, and circumstances were strategically and serendipitously positioned along my path—sometimes for the purpose of making both my life and their lives better.

Today, I refuse to return what the followers of Jim Crow rendered unto to me. In fact, it has been my most fervent desire to find ways to somehow enrich their lives as well.

Today, as I look around my world and the worlds of those who are dear to me, I take stock of my daily peace, calm, and joy, but I also recognize that this peace, calm, and joy results from my new way of thinking and also from my attempt to foster peace, calm, and joy in the lives of those around me.

Today, I am no longer that maladjusted, angry young man from a segregated neighborhood in Montgomery. Instead, I am driven by an insatiable quest to identify opportunities to serve my community. I am convinced that my community's successes are inextricably tied to mine, and mine to theirs.

Today, I embrace the world through my artistic lens. I tend to see all the world—all of life in fact—as something of a canvas. The concerns and cares of life cover so many dimensions. They virtually plead for thoughtful, imaginative, and colorful brushstrokes of creativity and design. Each day I look forward to extending my creative reach and to utilizing those mediums that are readily at my disposal. I dip my virtual paint brush into relationships, circumstances, challenges, struggles . . . good and bad, but especially the bad—and paint a new day. This practice allows me to add more color and definition to the masterpiece we call life.

I believe that a series of fundamental thought patterns led to such thinking and achievements. These were patterns of thinking that, although uniquely powerful enough to free me from the grip of Jim Crow and the poison of self-hate, are bountifully available to all of us. But it takes an awareness of these thought patterns to reap their benefits. So the real question becomes: "What is it that I see . . . when I see you? . . . What is it that you see . . . when you see me?"

Are we willing to deal honestly with our answers to such a piercing question?

When we see others in terms of age, gender, sexuality, abled-ness, ethnicity, housing status, intelligence, education, or financial status, what is it that we see . . . really? That is perhaps one of the most basic and fundamental, one of the most honest, significant, and innermost personal questions that we can ask ourselves—one that ought to conjure genuine internal debate in our most sincere quest for calibrating and righting our vision of others.

Having honestly put that question to ourselves, now we can more readily challenge ourselves to develop relationships with people who do not look like ourselves, who do not think like ourselves, who do not believe as we believe. We can do this in the most fervent effort both to extend our and to embrace their personal resource capital and reach!

For that reason I have put pen to paper, hoping that future generations might find something worth considering in the pages that follow. I wrote this book for my family, but in the end we all are our brother's keeper. And so this book was written for you as well. As you will read in the chapters to come, so many people, over the years, kept the faith for me. With these words, I keep the faith with you.

1

WHY NOT WIN?

It was sometime in the mid-1980s—I don't recall the exact year—and the Boston Celtics were again playing the Los Angeles Lakers in the NBA Finals. And although I was 2,000 miles away, watching the game on the local CBS station in Birmingham, I was on the edge of my seat. Would this be the year that the Lakers—led by Kareem Abdul-Jabbar and Magic Johnson—finally beat Larry Bird and the Celtics?

While the teams were preparing to exit the locker room and I was bracing for what I was sure would be the game of the century, the camera panned onto a nondescript piece of sports philosophy affixed to the wall. The thirteen words of copy will resonate with me for the remainder of my days:

The game has been scheduled,
so we have to play.
Why not win?

Those three lines of commentary have weighed upon the very core of my existence. They challenge the primordial and existential aspect of my very being—and, I venture, will challenge yours as well. When you're a serious player, you can't just show up to a game. If you are going to sweat, risk injury, and endure the jockeying for position, you might as well win. Those words sat with me for a moment and then began to reverberate in my mind, but on a slightly different frequency. What if one took that same approach to life, but with another set of thirteen words:

You have now been born,
so you have to live.
Why not win?

As I reflected, I realized that that was exactly what I had thought to do in my life. As a young man years ago, I stood at a crossroads. I was unsettled, poor, and with no visible path toward progress. But after a teacher gave me a life-altering admonition that I'll share later, I picked up the ball of life and got into the game. And not just to play, but to win.

What if more of us did that: made up our minds to take the life that we are given and—no matter the fumbles or the fouls—make the most of it and resolve to win? In the same way that a basketball star gets into the game and uses his every talent and tool to win the game, we should do that with life.

And, if we are going to win in life, we've got to make it our mission to really go after the ball—no passive, apathetic, lackadaisical, mediocre, lukewarm, commonplace, ordinary, or everyday approach will do. If we are going to work to win, we've got to be motivated, excited, passionate, dynamic, and enthusiastic.

"Enthusiastic"—now there's a word for you. Someone once said that nothing great was ever achieved without it. And enthusiasm, like those other traits I listed, can be developed within any and all of us.

Years ago, I took a Dale Carnegie course sponsored by Coca-Cola. We began each meeting with a pep rally of sorts. We would roll up a newspaper like a bat and beat it into the palms of our hands to the rhythm of this mantra: *"Act enthusiastic, you'll be enthusiastic. Act enthusiastic, you'll be enthusiastic."* In other words, you may not feel excited, passionate, or enthusiastic, but it's all in the act! Pretty soon, your brain will catch up, and the results will follow.

My life, like most, has been filled with setbacks, stalls, and false starts. Because of my zip code, skin color, and grades in school, people thought I at best could only be a benchwarmer in the game of life. For a time, I even thought that myself. But even if I got tripped, I continued to get up, get in, and go after the ball again. I was determined, until the buzzer sounded, to continue my efforts to score. There is something about getting back up after embarrassments, humiliations, and wounds that makes winning that much sweeter. Believe me, I know.

Winning in life isn't necessarily aligned with having lots of money, all the right connections, or all the appropriate degrees. You and I know individuals who have MBA diplomas hanging on their office walls but who couldn't run a lemonade stand. On the other hand, I have an art degree—hardly the traditional foundation for business success—but nevertheless serve on corporate boards, fly on private jets to serve on international committees, and own multiple restaurants with twenty-five years of success behind me.

So what's the difference?

The difference, I think, is pushing beyond just participating in the game of life to constantly maneuvering to take the winning shot. And, when you win, it is very important to understand that the win is not just for you, but for those around you. When you win, your whole team wins. And what's even better, I think, is that, unlike in athletic contests, there doesn't have to be a loser on the other side of each of your victories.

I know that I will never win a championship ring for basketball. But when it comes to the life I have been given, I have absolutely no intention of quitting. I am determined to win all the days of my life, for me, for my family, and for others. And, in the end, I'm convinced that my will to win means that I will indeed win.

To my son, I would say: There's a ball with your name on it. You may drop the ball and others may try hard to take it from you, but never forget that it's yours. Hold on tight, get in the game, and play to win.

2

HUMBLE BEGINNINGS
BREED HUMILITY FOR A LIFETIME

Growing up, I didn't think that I was necessarily positioned to win. I grew up in a poor, but close-knit community called Madison Park, which was founded by fourteen former slaves and named after its leader, Eli Madison. My father, Arthur, was a baker at the VA Hospital, and my mother, Sarah, managed the lunchroom at my elementary school. They raised their five children on a very modest income.

Every winter, as families used improperly ventilated wood-burning stoves and open fireplaces to keep their homes warm, it was not a question of *if* someone's home would burn down. Rather, it was a question of which one. I remember vividly the day my friend Hosea's house caught on fire. His baby sister was trapped inside. His horrified mother was helpless to fight the flames, and we all stood stunned as she rolled around on the ground, clawing and screaming while calling out her baby's name. By the time a fire truck reached our community from the distant fire station, it was too late.

That's the way it was for us. It never occurred to me at the time that in other communities homes had smoke detectors, were built with flame-retardant materials, and had a fire station only a short distance away. We weren't so lucky.

How do you even imagine winning in an environment like that?

The summer brought its own perils. It was never a question of *if* a child would drown. Every summer, it seemed, one would; sometimes more than one. Madison Park was in an area that was exploited by rock and gravel companies; their depleted quarries were left abandoned and unfilled. When it rained heavily, the large pits would fill up with water and, in our young eyes, they became swimming pools.

One day, two brothers who lived right next door to me were tossing their ball near one of the pits. It fell into the makeshift pool. Not wanting to lose his only ball, the younger brother, Chris, went in to get it, but, of course, he did not know how to swim. Where was one going to learn to swim in Madison Park? In segregated Montgomery, there were no swimming pools for African Americans. But the water was deeper than Chris expected and his struggles quickly turned to panic. His older brother, KeeKee, jumped in to save him. The pit was too deep, and the water too vast. Both drowned.

What mother could sustain her hope and sanity after that kind of loss? How could she win? How could she even imagine winning?

Such stories happened regularly in our community. Other classmates were hit by cars as we walked unchaperoned along the miles-long trek to our school that was located across a major highway. They perished trying to maneuver their tiny bodies in and around speeding vehicles.

In Madison Park, tragedy was always knocking, it seemed. "Winning" was a foreign word, and it seemed we were marked for tragedy just because we were poor. It would have been easy for my parents, and even me at that young age, to see ourselves as branded for inevitable calamity.

Something Special

But my mother did not see it that way—or at least she managed to see beyond Madison Park. She saw hope in me. She would take my hands, examine their lines, angles, and fingernails, and say, "These hands are going to do something special someday."

Her words would give me a burst of fresh air. For a moment, anyway.

But then, I would often wonder how she could reasonably, not to mention realistically, imagine such a thing.

The funny thing was that she wasn't the only one possessed with what seemed like unrealistic hope. There was actually a lot of it in Madison Park. Just like our ancestors who had plowed that land before us, we all made the best of what we had. Neighbors and community folks enclosed a baseball park by nailing corrugated metal panels to wooden poles. We would play for hours. We even created a team we called the Blue Sox. After a long week of hard labor, the families would gather to host cookouts and share stories of the day. They'd laugh, eat fried fish and hot dogs, and, for a moment, forget about the drownings, the fires, the insufficient paychecks, and the turbulent times around us. And, most importantly to me, the tooth fairy knew how to find us. I remember fondly the joy of losing a tooth, putting it under my pillow and waking up to find a shiny nickel, dime, or quarter in its place. That was big money in that day. To a kid, it was magical how the coin would appear from out of thin air.

One day, my friends Ronnie and Eddie and I went hunting for muscadines. In the course of our wanderings, we came across a skull. It might have been that of a large dog or maybe even a cow; we weren't quite sure. But we did know one important thing—that bleached skull had a head full of teeth! We gleefully took it home, got out a hammer and some pliers, and divided up the molars.

Each of us put several of the teeth underneath our pillows, thinking that we would awaken to a pile of shiny coins. The next day, however, those same teeth were still lying there. We wracked our brains until we figured out where we went wrong: we had forgotten to notify the tooth fairy.

Like I said, we were a community full of hope!

Feasting on the Bread for Pigs

He wasn't the tooth fairy, but Mr. Richard Fuller was the closest thing to it in Madison Park. He owned a large farm and grocery store across the bridge. If someone in the community needed anything, from lunch money for school to a loaf of bread to accompany the night's dinner, he was the man to see. Mr. Fuller, or "Uncle Buddy" as some folks called him, was a kind and gentle man. As long as he had provisions, so did his fellow African Americans in the surrounding community.

I remember that Mr. Fuller would get day-old bread—actually, it was more like seven- or eight-day-old—from bakeries across town and bring it back to his huge barn. The bread was food for his pigs. It wasn't strange, however, for people in the community to ask for some of the extra for their dinner tables. Bread was a treat that not everyone could afford on a regular basis.

Whenever we kids would see Mr. Fuller's truck pull up to the barn, we would run toward it in hopes of being among the first to get the freshest of the *old* bread. He never shooed us away; he would always welcome us. He had so much bread that it wouldn't make a dent in the mountain of loaves he had stored.

On those days when Daddy's pay had been stretched until all that was left was pocket lint, I would go—many times in the cold—the two or three blocks to Mr. Fuller's and say, "Mama said can I get some bread out of the bread house." Mr. Fuller was happy to oblige.

There was a huge metal padlock and chain on the barn door that made an eerie, screeching sound under the sway of its heavy weight and rusty hinges. He would give me the key and once inside, I would fish for loaves. I would squeeze the bread bags in search of the softest ones. If I stumbled upon a cake, a cinnamon roll, or a honey bun, that would be a special treat. And not once, while sifting through the food, did it dawn on me that this food was actually meant for pigs.

In my present line of work, as the owner of several McDonald's restaurants, I often think back to those days. My memories are tinged with no small degree of irony. For us, at McDonald's, the freshness of our hamburger buns is a very serious matter. Freshness is essential to the overall taste perception and profile of our sandwiches. We are driven, and drive our employees, to pay strict attention to coded dates and proper handling procedures. Our bun quality assurance and control efforts are worlds removed from my sifting through a pile of week-old bread at Mr. Fuller's pig farm.

Back then, on any given day, there could be others searching for bread alongside me. We never felt like losers standing in that sea of bread because Mr. Fuller made us all feel like winners. We were winners because to him we were human beings and that made us his brothers and sisters.

I would get a couple of loaves for our family, take them home, and once they were toasted and topped with a little butter, they tasted just fine. Instead of making lemons out of lemonade, we made toast out of week-old bread. My family was not singled out or made to feel bad. Mr. Fuller knew the condition of most of the community. I couldn't tell you the number of times we didn't have lunch money. I would go to him and say, "My mama wants to know if we could borrow thirty-five cents." He would give it, and how or if my parents paid him back, I don't know.

I will never forget Mr. Fuller's kindness. In so many ways, I've tried to be some modicum of a Mr. Fuller. I have tried to be a Mr. Fuller for the people in my life. I never let myself forget that, with much pride, I ate the food meant for pigs.

To my young cousin, I would say: No matter how many opportunities or accolades you receive, or whether your beginnings are humbled or privileged, you can never give "too much" to others in genuine need. Who was it that said, "Where much is given, much is required?" That is how you really win—by giving to others and setting them up to be winners as well.

3

IF YOU CAN'T TAKE ANYTHING . . .

So often, it seems the things that happen to us in life are not so much about what is happening in the moment, but rather are about placing us on a path to lead the way for others.

It would be years before I realized the truth of that.

First of all, consider that I was born in 1954. That was a big year for my parents, but an even bigger one for the United States. Dwight Eisenhower was president. Bill Haley and the Comets released "Rock Around the Clock," which ushered in the era of rock and roll. *Sports Illustrated* released its first issue, with the Milwaukee Braves' Eddie Mathews at bat on the cover. The Dow Jones Industrial Average hit a record high—of 382.74 points. The world's first nuclear submarine, the USS *Nautilus*, launched; the world's first Boeing 707 flew. In my home state of Alabama, a meteorite even hit a human being—an unfortunate woman named Ann Hodges—for the first time in recorded history.

And, in Washington, D.C., on May 17, 1954, the U.S. Supreme Court released its opinion in the landmark case, *Brown v. Board of Education of Topeka*. The Supreme Court, which counted among its members Alabama's own Hugo Black, voted 9–0 to reject the "separate but equal" educational system of Topeka, Kansas, and the four other locales in the consolidated litigation that led up the decision. "We conclude that, in the field of public education, the doctrine of 'separate but equal' has no place," Chief Justice

Earl Warren wrote for the unanimous court. "Separate educational facilities are inherently unequal."

Brown v. Board of Education turned public education on its head from Texas to Delaware, from Missouri to Florida, and, of course, ultimately, in Montgomery. But, for me, those days were still in the future.

Elementary School

In 1959, while a student at Madison Park Elementary School, I skipped the first grade and went from kindergarten straight to second grade. I was five years old in a classroom full of seven- and eight-year-olds. I was rather intimidated, but art became the refuge in my little world. I fell in love with it, thanks to my teacher, Mrs. Cook. She was something of an artist, and her brown beauty, in my young eyes, made her a work of art in her own right.

With each new holiday or season change, Mrs. Cook would use colored chalk to sketch on the blackboard amazing drawings such as the Horn of Plenty, the Easter Bunny, and Santa Claus. When my class would go outside for recess we'd return to a display of her wonderful creations. It was like magic. I was so impressed that one day I asked if I could stay in and watch. Fortunately, she said yes.

During those afternoon sessions, while my classmates were outside running and swinging, I would study her wrist as she made strokes on the chalkboard, and I memorized the forms of the loops and swoops of her sketches. I tried to absorb it all and, without being fully aware, I became saturated with a keen fascination for all things artistic.

As the years went by, my artwork became a little better, although sadly, life for African Americans did not. For us, life in the South during the 1960s was not a pretty picture. It was ugly and raw, with hard lines and jagged edges. *Brown v. Board of Education* had outlawed public school desegregation back in 1954, but Alabama lawmakers and law enforcers seemed to view the U.S. Supreme Court's decision as merely a recommendation, not a requirement. Alabama's children continued to go to schools separated along racial lines as our legislators worked with almost diabolical creativity to avoid the *Brown* mandate. In fact, it took a series of federal district court rulings in Alabama, starting with *Lee v. Macon County Board of Education* in 1963, to really start unraveling Alabama's segregated school system. In the meantime, the Civil Rights Act of 1964, which prohibited school boards from depriving students of the equal protection of the laws based on their race, color, religion or national origin, gave more federal teeth to the fight for equal education.

Solomon Seay, an African American attorney who lived in Madison Park (in fact, his maternal great-grandfather, Eli Madison, had founded Madison Park), led the fight in our community. He and his law partner Fred Gray had successfully litigated the *Lee* case, and he felt strongly that blacks should take advantage of these new freedoms to attend the so-called "white schools." Although it might seem strange to a reader today, virtually all of the people I knew were content to stay in all-black schools, even if it meant continuing to accept segregation. None of us saw the benefit of leaving the comfort and familiarity of our classrooms to learn alongside people who had historically rejected us.

And besides, we knew what trying to integrate could mean in Alabama. Tuscaloosa, Autherine Lucy had tried to become the first black student to enroll at the University of Alabama back in 1956; threatened with ever-growing mobs who pelted her with rotten eggs and hurled vile profanity at her, she only lasted through three days of classes. The next year, in 1957, when civil rights leader Rev. Fred Shuttlesworth had the temerity to try to enter two of his daughters at Birmingham's all-white Phillips High School, angry white hoodlums beat him nearly senseless.

In 1963, when African American students again tried to register at the University of Alabama, they were confronted with the spectacle of Governor George Wallace "standing in the school house door" to try, unsuccessfully, to block their admission. But in Birmingham a few short months later, the Ku Klux Klan seemingly retaliated to this and other defeats by bombing the Sixteenth Street Baptist Church, killing four little girls who had done nothing other than to attend Sunday School.

In short, in 1967, integrating schools in Alabama in the shadow of Jim Crow was serious business, and for a twelve-year-old like me, there was little appeal in picking such a fight.

But Attorney Seay claimed that inside the walls of those "white schools" were better classrooms, better books, and better resources. If we were going to create leaders in our community, he argued, we needed to position our people to take advantage of everything that was available.

Seay went around knocking on people's doors and canvassing the community for participants in an integration program. He told the folks of Madison Park that the schoolhouse door was open for us and that we needed to walk on in. After much cajoling, Seay persuaded the parents of at least six children (including his daughter, Sheryl) to integrate the all-white Goodwyn Junior High School. By some strange luck—or curse as I thought at the time—I was one of them.

Going to Goodwyn

There we were: Ronnie, Eddie, Sheryl, George, Horace, Loiss, and me, standing on the side of the street in Madison Park. On that late summer morning in 1967, we were six wide-eyed black youngsters, dressed and ready to leave behind everything we knew for our new school across town.

As we waited, I remember asking myself: "Why had my mother volunteered me to experience this impending torment?" My homies were at all-black Booker T. Washington Junior High, where we had spent seventh and eighth grades together. Now, I was being plucked out to spend ninth grade at Goodwyn. What had I done to deserve this? I took it personally. My October birthday would have made me younger than most of my classmates anyway, plus I had skipped first grade, so I was entering ninth grade at age twelve. My mind couldn't appreciate at the time that there was a bigger picture, that I was a part of a greater cause to help black people get what they needed, and now was my time to lean in and lend a hand to that struggle. If I could go back and talk to my twelve-year-old self, I would say, "This experience is not about you. I know you are young. I know you are afraid, but if you conquer this, the ripple effects will touch your children, your children's children, and a Southern community beyond imagination."

It would take me many years to realize those truths and, in the meantime, a big yellow school bus was approaching us. It pulled to the side of the road and, as the six of us climbed aboard, everyone who lived in Madison Park watched and prayed. We squeezed into a cluster of seats amid a sea of curious white faces and steeled ourselves to enter their world.

To my eyes, Goodwyn was a strange world of white folks. Every day, from the moment we got off the bus in the morning until we were back on in the afternoon, we were often belittled, dismissed, humiliated, and sometimes pinched, pushed, and shoved. To say those were challenging times would be the epitome of an understatement.

For example, if I took a drink of water from the hall fountain, then, for the rest of the day the white students would refuse to drink after me because that water spout had been "contaminated." My taking a seat at a particular table in the lunchroom was cause for the white students to move to another. In phys ed, I was never picked for a team; the coach would have to assign me to one. And if by some rare circumstance I got the ball, no one wanted to touch me. I would be allowed to make an easy touchdown while my white classmates laughed.

Other gestures were less overt but in the long run maybe even more damaging. In the classrooms, white students would not sit within five feet of me. Clearly, in their eyes, I was academically inferior, and they were not going to take any chance of my inferiority rubbing off onto them. That was a lot for a twelve-year-old to process. Unsurprisingly, I began to hate school and everything and everyone associated with it. My mother had sent me to Goodwyn to learn, but instead of getting a lesson in math, science, or reading, I was getting schooled in my worthlessness and inferiority.

"Y'all's King Is Dead"

I still remember Friday, April 5, 1968. It was the day after Dr. Martin Luther King Jr. was assassinated in Memphis. My family and community were heartbroken, but the folks at Goodwyn felt differently. That next morning as our bus pulled up to the school, a feeling of foreboding gripped our small group of Madison Park students.

The white kids gathered in a mob at the entrance of the bus. They looked bloodthirsty, anxiously waiting to see our faces and revel in our response. Inside the bus, we were dead silent as we braced ourselves to face them. I would imagine that our breathing slowed and our muscles tensed. When the vehicle stopped, our group slowly exited with a somberness that mirrored that of a funeral.

"Y'all's king is dead," belted out a little freckle-faced white boy. "What y'all niggers gonna do now?"

Lois Boswell, who was sort of a fiery girl, snapped back: "And y'all's queen is dying. What *y'all* gonna do?" She was referring to Lurleen Wallace, the governor of Alabama, who was dying of cancer. Does matching vitriol with vitriol ever prove beneficial? I think not! But that pretty much did shut up Freckle Face and his crowd.

Despite such rallying moments, life at Goodwyn took its toll on our small band of pioneers. Some students, like George, who is still my good friend today, were pulled out of Goodwyn by their parents. And who could blame those parents? Who could blame George? Who would purposely endure what we endured if they didn't have to?

The next year, having barely survived Goodwyn, I found myself at an essentially all-white high school—ironically named after Confederate General Robert E. Lee. There were some signs of progress. Each year, Attorney Seay had continued to recruit more and more blacks to integrate Montgomery schools. And as more of us entered the previously all-white public schools, sports and other activities began to iron out some of the great divide between the races. As we became more accustomed to each other, circumstances began to get a little better year after year. The tensions seemed to lessen, and our daily interactions with the white students seemed to improve. My grades, unfortunately, did not.

After my first year at Goodwyn, I had to go to summer school because I had failed several subjects. Once I reached the tenth grade at Lee, the failings continued. At that point, trying to earn a high school diploma seemed insurmountable. I had begun to shut down. But I was too young to drop out of school, and my mother definitely was not going to let that happen, so I was stuck. For me, high school was a series of frustrating defeats. I went to summer school every year, and by the time I became a senior, my class was preparing to graduate and advance to college or take vocational jobs without me. My fate as a loser was being cemented, I believed.

At the time, I was also working at the Majik Mart, a local convenience store. Although I was too young to work that job legally because we sold alcohol, the owner overcame that hurdle by simply paying me in cash. My pay was less than the other workers, but I was absolutely thrilled to be making my own money.

Like any neighborhood store, the Majik Mart had its collection of regular customers. One who never strayed from his routine would come in for his daily Schlitz Malt Liquor purchase between five and six in the afternoon. With a cavalier demeanor, he would slap a six-pack on the counter and recite his rather mundane and trite mantra, "Another day, another dollar. You and me ain't gonna never have shit in life. You know what I'm saying, bud?"

Without any thought, I would respond, "I think you're right."

I saw no evidence for reasons to disagree with him. And that put me on a dangerous road. Not only was I perpetuating a negative perception of myself, but I was also buying into this man's declaration that neither of us could or would amount to anything.

Meanwhile, back at Robert E. Lee High School, I trudged into my final session of summer school. With my poor academic record and no prospects, it was, for me, a daily walk of shame. Nevertheless, I was determined to complete this journey—if not for me, then at least for my mother. And, whether I knew it or not, I had learned valuable lessons both at Goodwyn and at Lee.

When I think back on my experiences at those schools, I can truly say that although it was painful, it wasn't for naught. All of life is about getting ready. We learn to crawl in preparation to walk. We master walking so that we can prepare to run. As crazy as it sounds, Goodwyn and Lee prepared me for a life I had no idea I would lead. Being in those all-white settings gave me a foundation for the life I am leading today: being the first and only African American in a number of boardrooms and sitting at a number of exclusive tables to make important decisions while looking around at faces that do not look like mine. Had I not learned at Goodwyn and Lee the lessons and the nuances of functioning in the unfamiliar world of white folks, I might not have been able to function in the world I live in today; in essence, I learned to be comfortable in uncomfortable settings.

These were big lessons. Even more surprisingly, however, my biggest lesson would be learned in the year to come—and from a most unlikely source.

To my son, I would say: If you can't take anything, then you can't have anything. The more you can take, the more you can have. I had to learn how to keep my eyes on the prize as the rewards of life are reserved only for those who stay in the game.

4

'OLD BATTLE AXE'

In my senior year at Lee High School, I faced yet another challenge. I had survived the past years of racial unrest and endured the shame of my academic failings, but I still had to avoid Miss Nichols.

Miss Nichols, who taught senior English, was the talk of Lee High. A veteran of World War II, she had retired from the military to take a second career teaching. She was petite, her big glasses took up most of her face, and she looked like she drank lemon juice for kicks. Miss Nichols hardly smiled and wasn't much for small talk, so the students called her "Old Battle Axe." My most fervent prayers were that I could avoid Miss Nichols during my final lap through high school.

Of course, fate had a different idea.

I ended up with Miss Nichols not only for senior English but for session room as well. Surely, I thought, this was the nail in the coffin of my academic career. How could I survive Miss Nichols?

From the beginning, she lived up to her intimidating reputation. She seemed to have memorized our names overnight. She would stand at the door of her classroom, welcoming us individually by name to what we all believed would be our daily dosage of hell. I never made better than a C in that English class (and probably only one of those). I did receive a B+, however, on a book report on *Pilgrim's Progress* by John Bunyan. I was fascinated with the characters Love, Mercy, Hope, and Forgiveness. I've often reflected on that interlude.

But despite my struggles with literature, or perhaps because of them, Miss Nichols recognized my need to express myself with my art. Throughout my time at Lee, my only reprieve had been my art. Locked out of the white students' world, I had created my own universe with my pencil and the lined papers that should have been used for learning. I would get lost in the lines and dissolve into the circles. I guess the Battle Axe saw that need in me and, like all great teachers, found a way to harness it. Quite often, she would have me assist her with drawings for her bulletin board, bringing a sense of purpose and accomplishment to my otherwise grim days. That exchange happened for a while, and then, late in the school year, she asked me to assist her with some yard work at her home.

Miss Nichols's invitation didn't necessarily surprise me. I assumed that she wanted me to come to her home and do what my dad and I did most weekends: work in the yard at the "white folks' house." Their names were always incidental; they were just the "white folks." We would mow grass, rake leaves, and pull weeds practically all day. During break time, we would be treated to wax paper-wrapped sandwiches and paper cups of water passed out through the back door.

The experience at Miss Nichols's home, however, was different. I did the usual yard work, but during lunchtime she did something unthinkable. She invited me into her home. I was further flabbergasted when she had me come in through the front door. It was the first time, as I recall, that I had gone through the front door of a white person's home—ever.

Inside, Miss Nichols had prepared food for three. She lived with her sister. (It figured, I thought, rather meanly at the time, since what man would live with "Old Battle Axe"?) And there I was, having entered through the front door, now sitting at her dining room table. I ate from her china and silver and drank from her crystal. It was good food, as I recall, but the magnitude of the experience was difficult to digest.

On that afternoon, Miss Nichols shared choice nuggets of wisdom with me. I tried to hear her, but I was so busy listening to what she was doing that I heard little of what she had to say. As she spoke, I was simultaneously taking a tour of my past, which included visits with my mother to H. L. Green's Department Store in downtown Montgomery. In my memory, I saw myself longing for a hamburger and a glass of milk and moving toward the diner section—brightly lit, full of booth seats, bountiful green plants, and smiling faces. My mother would notice me eyeballing the food and would give me a slight tug. She would take me by the hand and lead me downstairs to a smoky bar with worn, rickety stools and a smelly grill. People with my skin tone had to sit on stools that creaked and eat food from paper plates instead of china. I have to admit that the memory haunts me to this day. For me, food is not just food. Presentation is everything. For years, I would keep a plate at my McDonald's restaurant from which to occasionally eat breakfast. Strangely enough, the food just tasted better that way.

Miss Nichols must have noticed my wandering thoughts, but she persisted in securing my attention and, with mystical clarity, said, "Larry, I think you should go to college."

College? This woman knew firsthand of my academic slips and failures and of my apathetic approach to learning. Why was she saying this to me? No one had even imagined, let alone mentioned, my name and college in the same sentence. But if anyone knew college material, surely Miss Nichols did. She was not one for embellishing. If she said it, she meant it. Before I knew it, the words of Old Battle Axe had begun to chop away my feelings of inferiority.

I left her home that day daring to think differently about myself. I remember sharing with my homeboys what she said to me, and in the easy comfort of those surroundings, we laughed at the absurdity of it.

Subconsciously, however, her dare to me to view myself differently began to turn from an absurdity to a welcomed challenge. I must admit that I always suspected, deep down, that I had something to offer. Something inside me had always been whispering that maybe there was potential inside of me. That internal voice, along with Miss Nichols's words, became the choir I needed to sing my salvation.

My way of thinking did not change overnight. The evolution of redirecting my thoughts, changing my approach, expressing my opinions, would happen over many years. But clearly the Miss Nichols experience had laid a foundation that provided a banquet of opportunity for me to win in life beyond what I could ever have imagined.

To my cousin, I would say: Shed the person inside yourself who sees you through a negative lens. Work to conquer your former self, and then allow the new you to conquer the world. Give yourself permission to be great.

5

DON'T BE AFRAID
TO UNWRAP YOUR GIFTS

Believe it or not, the kid—me—who went to summer school every year, failed classes, and barely escaped high school, ultimately enrolled at Alexander City State Junior College. Going to college had never even entered into my mind until my conversation with Miss Nichols in her home. It reminds me of the law of inertia: an object in motion stays in motion until acted upon by an outside force. I was moving steadily along a path of defeat and lack of motivation until the outside force that was Miss Nichols stopped me cold. That meeting arrested me and set me moving along an altered trajectory, one that I enjoy to this very day.

What if I had been too afraid to show up to her house? What if I had brushed off her words? I would have continued my movement toward something less than worthy of me. Because of the Miss Nichols experience, to this day I am careful of what I run away from because I might be so *unfortunate* as to get away from it.

I will put it another way—what if I had been afraid to unwrap my gifts?

To amplify what I mean, let me go back for a moment to Madison Park Elementary and my fourth-grade year. And to the most beautiful girl in the world—a young lady named Geraldine. Okay, so my world was pretty small. But I would have stacked Geraldine against all comers, seen or unseen, from all corners of the globe. She was the love of my young life. Put another way, I really, really, really liked her.

There was only one problem: my very good friend Melvin felt likewise.

Melvin and I did everything together . . . shooting marbles, catching tadpoles, and busting up ant beds. The latter was our particular shared specialty. As fate would have it, Melvin was taller, faster, and a couple of years older than me. In short, he was stiff competition for seven-year-old me in the battle to win Geraldine's heart. But I could do the one thing that Melvin could not. I could draw.

And so during one sunny day's recess period, I set out, under a cloak of secrecy, to draw out Geraldine's name in as fancy and as colorful a manner as I could conceive. I'm not saying that it would have given the old Baroque masters any sleepless nights worried about the competition, but, with her carefully scripted name gilded with red and yellow hearts pierced by Cupid's arrows, I thought it was my best work ever. I even impressed myself!

As I surreptitiously slipped my masterpiece onto Geraldine's desk, Melvin spied my handiwork—and I could tell he was worried. But before he could say anything, recess was over, and Geraldine returned to her desk to find what I thought would truly win her heart. She took the mysterious drawing and flitted around the classroom showing her creatively drawn name to the other girls. There was no mistaking the look on her face—SHE WAS IMPRESSED!

For a time, Melvin bit his tongue. But then he could stand it no longer. With a begrudging air of defeat, he cried out the painful truth, "Larry did it!"

Geraldine turned to me with a look on her face that did not need the employment of a single word to say what I wanted to hear. When the other girls rushed over to have me write their names so fancy as that, I had bad news for them.

"No, I can only write Geraldine's name like that," I declared gallantly. Once again—GERALDINE WAS JUST TOO IMPRESSED!

Now it was the perfect time to pen the most important document that any fourth grader ever wrote—and it had nothing to do with reading, writing, or arithmetic. If I remember correctly, it went something like this:

Dear Geraldine, I like you. I hope you like me too. Will you be my girlfriend? Please write yes or no on the dotted line:

. . . .

(Oh, yes, the line was indeed dotted—that was standard procedure, you see.)

I slipped the note—or should I say document?—to Geraldine. She took it home for her studied consideration, leaving me to endure a night that seemed to stretch into a week.

The next morning, Geraldine returned my note to my desk with her response. Melvin, of course, grabbed the note and opened it before I could. I guess that was just fine because, when he threw it on the floor, I knew well enough that Geraldine had answered affirmatively. It goes without saying that I was the happiest boy at Madison Park Elementary as Geraldine and I "made eyes" with one another the entire day.

From that day forward, our young hearts lived happily ever after—for about five weeks. We, of course, broke up for one reason or another and, in the end, Melvin and I were back to shooting marbles and terrorizing ants, ignored by a thoroughly unimpressed Geraldine, no doubt. But even today, the memory of Geraldine reminds me that your gifts just might win a heart for you, for a season . . . but you first have to unwrap them.

Now let me return to the narrative of my early college days. To a modern-day student, the circumstances of my attendance at Alexander City State Junior College probably seem less than ideal. They included, for example, a daily fifty-four-mile commute (each way; about a two-hour trip after picking up other students along the route) on one of the junior college buses from Montgomery, through Wetumpka and Eclectic, to Alexander City. But the long trip to and from school was merely incidental . . . as I was now obviously considered college material. And not just merely college material—I was studying art. My own sense of self was coming into the view, and it was obvious to both me and to just about everyone around me. I remember my mom in one of her social club meetings speaking of me to the other ladies in our home. It made my heart happy to witness her genuine sense of pride of having a son in college.

After two successful quarters at ACSJC, I had learned the rudiments of basic drawing skills, compositional layout/design, and the principal elements of design. I was now ready, in terms of my artistic skills, to study art at Alabama State University. And while still not necessarily prepared academically, my enhanced self-esteem and passion, stoked by my developing artistic skills, catapulted me forward to ASU.

Admitted to ASU, I was now officially attending a university and, looking in the mirror, I found this new and improved "me" that was steadily evolving to be . . . quite agreeable! Soon after I arrived on campus at ASU and settled into the school's art department, the chairman, Dr. John Hall, recruited me to his department's work-study program as a commercial artist for the yearbook and athletic department. Participation in the program covered the cost of my tuition and books; in return, I practically lived in the art department. Winning awards in art competitions, perfecting the art of calligraphy, and being assigned to work with participating artists-in-residence happily became commonplace for me.

In many ways, however, I was a typical undergraduate student. A few years ago, I had a chance to reflect on my days as an ASU student when, as the school's chairman of its board of trustees, I was flying to Maryland to personally interview the educator we were recruiting to become the university's first female president, Dr. Gwendolyn Boyd, and to encourage her to accept our offer of employment. As I winged northward, I marveled at the contrast between the present—being ultimately responsible for hiring the new president of my alma mater—and the past. In those days of my youth, if any of my fellow students or I ever saw the president, Dr. Levi Watkins, coming from the right, we would instantly take an immediate left. We were not troublemakers—not in the least. But we saw absolutely no benefits in risking an engagement with the university's president. So I had progressed from avoiding the ASU president to hiring one of his successors. It's true . . . your gifts will indeed make a place for you.

My graduation from ASU was a particularly resonant moment for me. Standing in a sea of black and gold (the school colors) and dressed in my cap and gown, I thought of my mother. I reflected back on my young childhood when I heard her cry for the first time. It was a foreign sound to me because she was always so strong. But that day she was sobbing.

Worried, I tiptoed to her doorway and peeked into her room where she sat on her bed. She was weeping so hard that her face was buried in her hands. As she cried, interjecting the occasional mumbled word or prayer between sobs, I discerned that my older brother had done something—something so bad that it had broken her heart. Before she could see me, I ran back to bed, covered myself in my blanket, and promised that I would never be the one to make my mother cry.

At my graduation, however, I broke that oath.

After I walked across the stage to receive my college degree, I made my way to my mother and saw tears in her eyes. She was crying, but they were tears of joy because she was so proud of her baby boy. These hands that she had said would do something special had received a college degree.

That was one of my last memories of her. She died later that year in 1975.

I know that it was because of my mother and so many others that I had been able to reach that point. While I was in college, there were those earlier days when I would have to drop my father off at work, pick up his—not mine, *his*—paycheck, and take it over to my school to pay my tuition. Every day, he awoke, dressed, and worked hard—sometimes at two or three jobs—so that I could sit in a classroom and learn. Who would not be humbled by that kind of sacrifice and love?

Very little of anything of great significance is ever accomplished alone. Being aware of that principle has catapulted me to incredible levels. Whether personally, professionally, spiritually, or emotionally, winning is easier with the support of others. And it's not just recognizing that, but acknowledging it.

I heard someone say, "If you're ever walking down a country road and notice a tortoise on top of a fence post, you'll know he had a lot of help getting there." That parable is so true for most anyone of measurable success. This very basic and fundamental truth has stood the test of time. It defies argument or debate, yet I marvel at how few ever learn to leverage the help that's all around them and is usually theirs for the asking.

That was a lesson I learned at graduation—and one that I would have to rely upon again and again throughout my life.

They Took "Their" Job

After having acquired my bachelor's degree, there was no question what I would do as a career. Educators had shaped my life, so I was going to be a teacher. Toward the end of my senior year at ASU, I was recruited to apply for a teaching position at Vestavia Hills High School. I was successful and in 1975 moved to Birmingham to teach art in an affluent suburban community. And, fresh out of college, I was determined to be that cool educator whom everyone liked.

That was a big mistake.

At Vestavia Hills, I was far too familiar with my students. In fairness to everyone, I was very close to my students' own ages, and that proved more than I could handle. I became more of a buddy to my students than a teacher. They called me "Mr. T," and I was too busy "high-fiving" and being cool to gain the respect I needed in the classroom.

At the end of that year, my principal called me in for a conference. He began by telling me what an asset I was to the system. He knew I had, for example, spent hours painting backdrops for school plays and penning calligraphy on special awards and certificates. But then, with great tact and diplomacy, he advised me that when I returned in the fall, he expected me to be a teacher to my students—and not their friend. I was there to be the former, not the latter, and he expected to have a *teacher* report back for school in the fall.

With this strong direction and another year's worth of maturity, I began to settle into my role. I went on to teach fine arts and ceramics for four years, constituting one of the most rewarding periods of my career.

Working on Myself

As a first-year teacher, students would often ask me to sign their yearbooks. Unfortunately, I had no idea that I was drafting congratulatory statements riddled with typos and grammatical errors. They were so bad that, finally, a student approached me and said, "I can't believe you wrote that."

I was humiliated.

But instead of letting those words shame me into hiding, I began to work on this aspect of my life. I made reading books part of my daily discipline and I set a goal of learning two new words a day. I bought or borrowed books on the proper use of the English language, listened to newscasts, and practiced how to properly pronounce words like "often" and "salmon." In short, I went to work.

Then a funny thing happened. Just as had occurred with art, I fell in love with language. Words became like music to my ears. I loved their sounds and the tickle of their tones on my tongue, like with "utopia," "ubiquitous" and "duplicitous." Not only was I teaching, I was learning. Author and motivational speaker Jim Rohn said, "Work harder on yourself than on any job." That's what I had planned to do—and still do to this day.

It might not be a bad idea if more of us would deliberately strive to learn that extra word, read that extra book, improve our attitude, enhance our relationship skills, watch our demeanor, lose that extra pound, walk that extra mile, drink another glass of water, pass on that second slice of pie, and say "please," "thank you," and "excuse me" more often. When you create a better you, everyone gets a better you, including your students, colleagues, family, and community. What an awesome philosophy of thinking.

For me, these are not just hollow words. Even as I began to work on this book, years after my teaching days were over, I started taking Spanish lessons. I would never have imagined the level of unifying excitement the simple exchange of a few pleasantries in Spanish would afford me and my Hispanic/Latino employees. And it was priceless to be able to say, for the first time, to the Spanish-speaking customer in front of me with four cases of Coca-Cola product in the checkout line, "*Muchisimas gracias por comprar nuestros productos Coca-Cola*"—"Thank you very much for buying Coca-Cola."

I guess the old saying is right: "A mind that has been stretched by a new idea can never again return to its original dimensions."

I would have been content to be an educator for the rest of my life, but the State of Alabama disrupted my trajectory yet again. Sharp budget cuts affected schools across the state. At Vestavia Hills High School, art was one of the first to be sliced. In all, eight teachers had to go—and I was one of them.

The principal brought me into his office and said, "Larry, of all of the teachers I am losing, you are the most difficult to have to tell." He told me how I had done a great job, but that they just didn't have funding for two art teachers. He was a kind and caring man and it seemed to pain him to express that I was being let go. In fact, he had lined up two job interviews for me so that I could land on my feet.

It wasn't personal. There was no funding. But that event sent me into a mental shutdown. Teaching school was the only profession that I had ever planned for. I loved teaching. And now it was being snatched from me. In my mind, I revisited other disappointments. I thought back to the daily indignities of growing up in Madison Park. I reflected on being pulled out of my own comfortable school surroundings and being bused to Goodwyn Junior High. I remembered being left behind by my Lee high classmates my senior year as they graduated and I graduated later that summer. I even recalled my regular customer at the Majik Mart and his daily litany of defeatism. Maybe he was right after all.

Eventually, most of the other teachers who left Vestavia Hills found jobs teaching in other districts or in the corporate community. But I did not. I languished, feeling stunted, stuck, and torn.

At the time, I was looking for something to save me or give me direction as to the next steps. In truth, the only place I really needed to look was in a mirror.

When I think back on that experience, it reminds me of the story of the Wizard of Oz. So often we search high and low for the answers to what direction we need to take in life, but we already have the answers inside. Remember Scarecrow? He wanted a brain. The Tin Man needed a heart. The Lion desired courage. They were waiting on the Wizard to hand those things over to them, only to learn that they, like all of us, already possessed those very same traits.

You don't need permission from the Wizard to operate in the gifts you already have. The Lion could not have challenged the Wicked Witch if he didn't have courage. Just like him, I already had what I needed to move forward. I was disheartened at the thought of potentially not being able to practice as an artist because Vestavia Hills had taken away my job. But, as I realized later, Vestavia Hills had not made me an artist. I was an artist before that and could be an artist afterwards. I just needed to remind myself of that reality and accept that truth.

Quite often, we ourselves pose the greatest deterrent to our own well-being. From that experience, I fashioned a short prayer, to which, even to this day, I often turn: "Save me, O God, from that wretched man: my own self."

Most of us are blessed with five gifts. They are our senses—sight, sound, smell, taste, and touch. Unlike Stevie Wonder, who has eyes but whose eyes cannot see, the vast majority of us have sight. But, the question is, what are we looking at? What are we actually seeing? Unlike Helen Keller, we can hear, but what are we choosing to listen to? We have a mouth and a tongue to talk, but what are we talking about? We have legs that can walk, but where are we going?

Perhaps we should look inside often in search of how we might use our gifts more effectively. Your gifts will make a place for you.

But it is not enough to realize that we have those gifts. We have to realize we have those gifts while there is time to make the most of them. An experience that a family friend from Louisiana once shared with me reinforces that point. He told me about a visit by his high school JROTC unit to the infamous Louisiana State Penitentiary known simply as Angola. Located in Louisiana's West Feliciana Parish, Angola is the largest maximum-security prison in the nation. My friend's visit happened to coincide with an annual exhibit of drawings, paintings, sculpture, and crafts by prison inmates.

The artwork on display awed the visiting JROTC students. Again and again, the students commented in sheer amazement at the incredible talent that created the paintings and sculptures before them. The warden, who was accompanying the students on the tour, replied with an observation clearly jaded by a career of seeing thousands of wasted lives wash up on his maximum-security doorstep each year.

"Oh, our inmates are some of the most talented individuals that you'd find anywhere," he said. "But they don't seem to realize that—until they get here."

What an unfortunate circumstance for so many of us, whether literally incarcerated by the state or imprisoned by jails of our own fashioning. Whether literal or figurative, it is imprisonment all the same.

In the wake of the loss of my job in Vestavia Hills, I was probably well on my way to constructing my very own Angola. But then the assistant principal at Pizitz Middle School, a gentleman named Fred Jones, reached out to me. Fred heard about my slump and came to see me.

"Man, you are really letting this thing get to you," he told me. "You have got to move on with your life."

And he was right.

After serious sessions of soul-searching, like the Prodigal Son I came unto myself. I snapped out of my funk and remembered that I was the same person whose mama had told him he possessed "hands that would do something special." I was the same one Miss Nichols saw as a college graduate. When I came unto myself, I realized that the school didn't take *my* job away, they took *their* job away. It was now up to me to go get *my* job.

To my daughter, I would say: Do not forget: your gifts will make a place for you. But you have to unwrap them first.

To my friend, I would say: Thank you for sharing your story about the prisoners of Angola. We must all allow our gifts to make a place for us while they matter and before it is too late for them to matter.

6

DRIVE THE RIGHT
BARGAIN WITH LIFE

After I lost "their" job at Vestavia Hills High School, the entrepreneurial bug bit me. Although I had no prior business experience, it made simple sense to me that I needed to find a way to work for myself so that I would never be in a position of losing someone else's job again.

So I started a freelance business painting signs for local companies. I had no experience working in a sign shop and nothing to go on but faith. I didn't have the right paint or the right materials, so I was constantly wearing out my brushes. I would paint on a wall with an acrylic brush when I should have been using fitches. But I was doing it nonetheless. Don't tell my lawyer friends this, but you don't have to wait for the proper documentation or for everything to be in place. You don't have to have all the i's dotted or all the t's crossed. You don't even have to be in the perfect starting position. Sometimes you just have to move in the right direction and learn as you go.

I started to have some success with the freelancing. I had clients such as Standard Furniture and Star Hardware. I was making it work. And, along the way, I would pick up tips like: "One Shot Paint is made for this kind of work." I would learn, adjust, and keep moving.

One day, I came upon a store called Cullatta's Grocery. I noticed that the Coca-Cola sign on the building was faded and so I asked the owner if

I could repaint it for him. The man told me that Coca-Cola painted that sign themselves and that it was free because he carried their product. I thought to myself, "Coca-Cola has a department that paints signs for free?"

By coincidence, I knew the president of the local Coca-Cola bottler because I had taught his daughters at Vestavia Hills High School and had also done a T-shirt design for him. I placed a call to him. When I got him on the phone, I told him what had happened and that I needed work. My real plan was to get into the Coke sign shop and learn to paint signs professionally. I only wanted to be there four to six months to get the training I needed and then get out of there to start my own business. Of course, I did not tell the president that, and happily he hired me over the phone and situated me in the sign shop. I was grateful for the opportunity.

When I arrived at Coca-Cola in 1979, I discovered that no one there could paint a sign as well as I could. Since the signs were free, customers weren't as critical of the end result, so the guys in the shop took advantage of the low bar that was set for them. I thought to myself, "Heck, I can't learn much here." Sign painting was something that I was pretty good at and I wanted my work to be great. For me, simply "OK" wasn't good enough. I was not going to stop until I became one of the best.

While working on signs, I would take Polaroids of my work and show them to some of the old sign masters—Tim Rock and Dave Skidmore—for critique. At first, they looked at me as if thinking, "We ain't never seen no black sign painter." But, nevertheless, they were very accommodating. I would take my pictures to them and they would give me tips such as to broaden the stroke and so forth.

Others, however, were not so tolerant. I was the only African American in the sign shop and, generally speaking, the other guys let me know in no uncertain terms that they were not necessarily happy about my being there. A couple would not speak when I said hello and, from time to time, would find ways to intimidate me or thwart my work. The year was 1979, and I suppose many of them had grown up in segregated communities and attended segregated schools. I doubt that there were more bad apples in that regard at Coca-Cola than at any other company in the South at the time—probably there were far fewer. Being an international brand, I suspect the situation at Coca-Cola was better than average.

Nevertheless, it almost felt like being at Goodwyn Middle School again. This time, however, I had a choice. I was not going to allow this situation to break me. Besides, I was only going to be here for a short period of time—just long enough to perfect my craft. Because I was something of a perfectionist when it came to my art, I would work around the clock, even coming in on the weekends. I would begin a sign and then start over. I would toil and tweak until it was nearly perfect in my eyes.

In those days, if you came into Coca-Cola after hours or on weekends, you had to sign a registry at the front desk. I noticed that on many occasions the only two names on the sheet would be mine and Claude Nielsen. I was a sign painter, and Claude was then the president and CEO of the company. Surely Claude must have wondered why I, some guy from the sign shop, was working on off days. My immediate boss certainly did. He would often ask me why I came in so much. "You don't own this company," he would say.

For him, I did not have much of a reply—at least at the time. It was true that I didn't own the company, but I did own my work ethic and my personal brand. I love quality and nothing that I touched was going to leave the shop until it was right. For me, the day or the time did not matter—I loved what I did and I was committed to perfection.

And today I receive a stock report from the company that reflects that I am indeed an owner of the company. I don't think that that outcome was unrelated to my attitude.

Every day, I was pursuing perfection with my work and trying to go the extra mile. That meant I wasn't just showing up to work, doing a job, and watching the clock. I realized that I was not working for Coca-Cola directly. Rather, I was working for life. Coca-Cola had only required me to come to work forty hours a week on a set schedule, but because I wanted more than what was expected, I gave more.

That reminds me of a Jessie B. Rittenhouse poem that I love:

I bargained with Life for a penny,
And Life would pay no more,
However I begged at evening
When I counted my scanty store;
For Life is just an employer,
He gives you what you ask,
But once you have set the wages,
Why, you must bear the task.
I worked for a menial's hire,
Only to learn, dismayed,
That any wage I had asked of Life,
Life would have paid.

In previous years, I had been that person who only expected the least of what life had to offer. I had bargained with life for a penny and a penny is what I got. But as I came unto myself, I renegotiated that deal. So, when I was working late and on weekends, I was not necessarily working for Coca-Cola. Instead, I was working for life. I bargained with life to make it a better place for me, my family, my community, and for everyone in it.

Of course, I was only going to realize a return on my investment if I upheld my end of the bargain. Life was ready to respond to the genuine sincerity of my efforts. It pains me to think of the number of people who miss their destiny for no other reason than a misunderstanding of this universal agreement between service and reward.

Later in life, I would discover the words and writings of Earl Nightingale, who spent his adolescence in a tent city in California during the
Great Depression, enlisted in the Marines at the age of seventeen, survived
the sinking of the USS *Arizona* at Pearl Harbor, and went on to become
one of America's great radio personalities and motivational speakers in the
post-World War Two era. Nightingale's thoughts and attitudes seemed to
articulate and reflect my own. Or perhaps it was vice versa. I don't suppose
it matters. But I recall him once saying that any person who is not satisfied
with his or her rewards has only to check his or her service.

I agree wholeheartedly. You'll get no better advice. It is as reliable as the
changing of the seasons.

> *To my nephew I would say: The world is not likely to respond to
> what we want, wish for, or even what we need. Rather, it responds
> only to what we deserve as a result of our most fervent efforts. The
> world waits to reward anyone who dares to insist upon being all
> that they can be. The universe is ordered, it seems, to respond with
> a corresponding reaction to our every action . . . therefore let your
> actions be good, thoughtful, positive, kind, sensitive, merciful,
> genuine, and sincere.*

> *To my cousin I would say: Be decisive when setting your bargain
> with life. Know that you can only get out of it what you are willing
> to put into it. A corporation, organization, or program may or may
> not pay you what you're worth, but life keeps accurate tabs and will
> always pay you exactly what you are worth (and not just in dollars
> and cents). Work for life and let life work for you.*

7

KNOW YOUR WORTH —
AND THE WORTH OF OTHERS

Ask yourself if you are willing to do more than you are paid to do. Today, it is as natural as breathing for me. I long ago discovered that when you do the bare minimum, you are only shortchanging yourself. Limited effort yields limited rewards. It really is that simple. So the question becomes, "Do we prefer a life of just working for a check, or would we prefer growth and development, personally and professionally?"

There is so much more than the proverbial dollar to be gained from this philosophy. I cannot think of anything that keeps more of us at the lower rungs of the ladder than being one who says, "I am not coming in one minute early, and I'm not staying one minute late. For what they're paying me, why should I?" It has been my experience that anyone who is not willing to do more than he or she is paid to do usually is not worth what he or she is being paid in the first place.

In my case, Coca-Cola had hired me, with a college degree, at $5 an hour. But I did not allow that starting wage to ruffle my feathers. Coca-Cola had no real idea of who they had hired, but I knew. And I was determined that it would only be a matter of time before they knew as well.

Where we start out, even if in a disadvantaged place or location, is not nearly as important as where we decide we are going. We should ask ourselves if we are are being viewed as a replaceable employee or an invaluable member of the team. Are we being viewed as an intricate part of the overall success of the organization? Even so, it is okay to start out as an hourly worker. I had started as a $5-an-hour sign painter. But with this newfound approach, I was well on my way to becoming someone the company would not want to replace.

If you're looking at the clock and saying, "Oh, my God, it is only ten o'clock—I have six more hours to go," then let that motivate you to re-position yourself on a pathway to a better experience. It may sound strange, but you know you have arrived when you are on the job and you look up at the clock and say, "Oh my, God, it's already two o'clock. I haven't done half of what I wanted to get done today." If you find yourself saying that, then it means you have been so busy doing what gives you purpose that time has flown by.

I remember when, shortly after I was hired, our sign department got a visit from Chester. Chester was an advertising manager from another one of Coca-Cola facilities and the gentleman who would be responsible for orienting me. At the time, the team and I were getting ready for a rodeo show by painting fifty-five-gallon barrels to look just like Coca-Cola cans.

Chester took a quick look at our work so far on the barrels, shook his head, and warned, "You know, if you do it that good and *they* see it, *they* are going to want it to look like that every time."

Clearly, "they," in Chester's mind, were our bosses and, to him, life was a zero-sum game. If *they* wanted something, then *we* were probably going to lose something. But that wasn't how I was looking at things. And although I didn't say it, I thought to myself, "If it *doesn't* look like this, then it *ain't* leaving the shop." It was obvious that the two of us had very different mindsets.

Eventually, word of the new designs being produced out of my shop made its way to the desk of the vice president of corporate marketing and communications. The man made a special trip to my department to inquire of their origin. He complimented their style and design and demanded to know who should be credited with these signs. I think it is fair to say that "Larry Thornton" was the last name he expected to hear.

After just four months of working at Coca-Cola in Birmingham, the company promoted me to advertising manager. The promotion took me by surprise. I wasn't looking to advance. Getting promoted was not part of my "six months and out" plan, but I had given them the best Larry I could be, and they had quickly seen me as someone who should be leading the way.

I've taken the position of never wanting to be more than I am, but I also never wanted to be less than I could be. Besides, being an advertising manager sounded like an interesting and exciting space to occupy. I accepted the challenge.

I remember my widowed father coming to visit me at work not long after my promotion. He was sitting in my office with me when several of my staff stepped in to report to me regarding one of our projects. My father just sat there in amazed silence until they left. Then he said, "Boy, you know you got a white man's job?"

In his own way, he was showering me with the highest praise. My father, who had lived in Madison Park for most of his life, attending segregated schools and riding segregated buses to work, had never seen and could not have imagined his own son having white men reporting to him.

My father was not the only one who would have to come to terms with such change. Several years later, Chester, the advertising manager who had cautioned me against creating designs that were too good, also faced change. Coca-Cola was discontinuing outdoor advertising at his particular sales center and he was given the option of early retirement, driving a route truck, or commuting forty miles each day to take a job reporting to me. Obviously, this was a difficult decision for him. He did not want to retire or drive a route truck. But having to report to the man he had previously trained would understandably be a blow to most anyone's ego.

As Chester wrestled with his impending decision, I could tell he was having a tough time. So I found a way to invite myself and my family to visit with him and his family at their lakeside home. It was a great afternoon of cooking-out, swimming, and fishing off his newly fashioned pier. He had a wonderful family who went out of their way to make my wife, my son, and me feel welcome. And, when the opportunity presented itself, I made a personal invitation for him to join my team in Birmingham. I told him that I did not have a management position for him at the time, but that I would really appreciate having his talent and experience as part of our aggressive advertising campaign. Coca-Cola was then in the middle of a sign war with our arch rival Pepsi that I felt quite responsible for initiating. It was a challenging time, but we were going to have fun, and if we were going to play, then why not win?

Chester did not give me an answer that afternoon but, as the day came to a close, his wife took a moment to quietly pull me aside and thank me for reaching out to them. My visit had put to rest her concerns for her husband's unpleasant dilemma, and in the end Chester agreed to come to Birmingham.

Once in Birmingham, Chester was a tremendous asset in our battle with Pepsi. The ultimate result was a win—for both of our families and for the Coca-Cola brand. As my career continued to develop, he went on to take my position as advertising manager, from which he recently retired.

The Most Important People on Earth

So often, we inadvertently discredit valuable human resources by insidiously practicing a childish game that I call the "too syndrome." It is harmful and counterproductive for children and it is just as harmful and ineffective for adults. We close people out and retard our own growth by making surface judgments of others' ability to contribute when we believe people to be: too fat or too skinny, too short or too tall, too smart or too dumb, too rich or too poor, too young or too old, too black or too white, and on and on and on. When we truly recognize the intrinsic value in everyone, we initiate an incalculable process of inclusion. This, in turn, fosters an economy of scale in human resources.

In his book *Lead the Field*, Earl Nightingale admonishes us to treat everyone we meet as if he or she was the most important person on earth. He says we should do that for three excellent reasons:

First, to everyone you meet, they are the most important person on earth.

Second, that's the way human beings ought to treat each other.

Finally, when we practice this approach, we set into motion a remarkable process for character development.

I still marvel at the profound truth of Nightingale's words, especially when we realize that essentially everything that will ever come to us will be through and by people.

In my own life, Miss Nichols could have easily looked no further than my academic missteps and in-school behavior and thought, "Larry is too dumb, too black, too unlearned, too far behind, and has too much of a chip on his shoulder about white people to amount to anything."

For my part, I easily could have looked at Miss Nichols and thought, "She is too old, too white, too mean, too demanding, and too steeped in our segregated cultures to care anything about me."

Chester could have looked at me and thought, "Larry is too focused on his own success to care about me."

I could have looked at Chester and thought, "Chester is too proud to ever want to join my team."

The president of Coca-Cola could have thought, "Larry is too inexperienced and too much of a loser to succeed in this company."

I could have looked at the president and thought, "He is too busy, too arrogant, and too biased to want to hire me."

Instead, we treated each other with the respect that we mutually deserved.

And what was the result?

Miss Nichols' faith in me was validated.

My trust in Miss Nichols was repaid with a lifetime of inspiration.

Chester's trust in my intentions was justified. He went on to finish a successful career with Coca-Cola.

With Chester joining us in Birmingham, my team was strengthened. We won the sign wars—at least by our estimation!

The president's confidence in me working for Coca-Cola was validated. He found himself a hard-working, innovative employee.

By being on Coca-Cola's team, I found a springboard for future business success.

In short, we all—Miss Nichols, Chester, the president, and me—thought in terms of "two," not "too." We took the time to think in terms of two people interacting with one another, not one person being "too" this or "too" that. And, in the end, the results spoke for themselves.

To my niece, I would say: Reach out and go out to people. Become comfortable in making the first move in developing new relationships. Those who can build and service relationships are victors. And remember—it is difficult to lock people out without, at the same time, locking ourselves in. Learn to appreciate that which is different and those who disagree with you. Welcome and learn to appreciate the inherent beauty in as many people as possible.

8

WORKING FROM YOUR CENTER

Some of the most exciting years of my career were spent as advertising manager in the sign department at Birmingham Coca-Cola. Graphic design, layout/composition, font selection, color coordinates, copy/illustration positioning—all offered up some of the most creative discoveries of my artistic experience. None were more exciting though, than working with the most recognized trademark in the world.

I must have drawn/painted/positioned the iconic Coca-Cola trademark literally thousands of times. My team and I started and ended each day committed to the lofty goal of positioning a Coca-Cola trademark within a one-mile range of every set of eyes in Birmingham. Whether working on a showcard, billboard, vehicle/transportation signage, or a mom-and-pop storefront, it never got too cold or too hot, too early or too late, or rained too hard to drown our enthusiasm for the completion of one more "red and white" experience. For my team, to paraphrase that famous Coca-Cola advertising slogan, "Coke was it."

I recall the amount of time we spent cutting our patterns, marking the guidelines, and oiling our brushes. In practically every instance—before sketching the layout, positioning the patterns, or the application of the first drop of red paint—the inarguable requisite for the conclusion of a successful sign experience was to . . . FIND YOUR CENTER! What an existential life message of paramount importance to all of us.

The use of guidelines and working from your center (as shown in the accompanying Coca-Cola illustration) provides the assurance of balance to the sign. If you start by finding the sign's center, then you take the guessing game of the "potential" for a successfully painted sign completely out of the equation. Instead, you can, with confidence, embark upon a virtually "guaranteed" success.

I always marveled in frustration at the amount of time I spent trying to convince some of my sign artists of this simple truth . . . and their wasteful obliviousness in ignoring these rules for successful sign artistry. I was appalled by how confident they were in starting their sign-painting exercise in total contrariness to this undisputed rule.

It might work, I would think, watching them wing it, but more often than not, they ended up wasting time, often having to start over . . . and again . . . and again, and frustrating themselves and me. And the sign resulting from such trial and error usually was far from presentable.

I think we as individuals likewise need to find our centers before embarking on our life's work. What centers us? What provides us with the vision and values that reveal a center against which to start painting our life story and against which to judge our subsequent strokes? What keeps us within the canvas and not disastrously scrolling off beyond the margins? Too many people lack that center; sadly, we can too often find examples of those un-centered souls even in our own families.

To my daughter, I would say: "Find your center and operate from it. Use, follow, adhere to the guidelines of life. They were meant to steer you toward successful living. In most instances, "attention" is all that you will have to pay. Surely you can afford that?

THORNTON

JUST A REMINDER!

9

THE WAY YOU RESPOND
CAN CHANGE SOMEONE'S WORLD

We can all learn a lesson from being too quick to look at a situation and shell out assignments or blame to others. But what might happen if we were, instead, more inclined toward self-assessment? What if we first looked inward for the solutions to our problems? What if *we* looked in the mirror more often to see what *we* could do to make a situation better or determine what *we* might have done that *we* did not do?

Self-awareness is key. My constant prayer has become, "Save me, oh God, from that wretched man—myself."

That was a virtue I had to exhibit shortly after I became the advertising manager for Coca-Cola in 1979. I had created a little makeshift office that was basically a cubicle with thin walls. There was not much room for anything but my desk and chair. But I did have room to affix a memo board to the wall.

One day, I walked into my makeshift office and noticed a small drawing in the lower corner of my memo board. I looked closer and saw that it was a tree with an outstretched limb. From the limb hung a rope that was tied around the neck of a silhouette of what appeared to be a black man. His head was twisted to the side. Beside the hanged man, a message read: "Just a reminder."

As I realized what I was seeing, the blood drained from my head down to my toes. For me, an image of a lynching was no mere metaphor of racism, even though I was, thankfully, a couple of generations removed from the heyday of such extrajudicial murders in the late nineteenth and early twentieth centuries. Despite the passage of those years, I knew that racial hatred still seethed in some hearts—and how sometimes it exploded to life. I knew, for example, what had happened to Emmett Till in Mississippi in 1955, a year after my birth, when the fourteen-year-old was accused of affronting a white woman. When local whites took justice into their own hands, Till's body ended up so battered and bloodied that a photo of him in his casket shocked the conscience of the nation. Yet his accused murderers were acquitted by an all-white jury after a mere sixty-seven minutes of deliberation.

The fact is that, although most people fail to appreciate it today, the U.S. Congress was never able to successfully pass an anti-lynching law—the kind of law that would have made such extrajudicial murders a federal crime, thus bringing federal wrath down on the perpetrators. I suppose that senators and newspaper editors and other opponents of such a measure had the luxury of arguing about infringements on states' rights and the wisdom of local mob violence being bested by local authorities—and they probably did not lose a whole lot of sleep about the absence of such a law. But when you grew up under a state-sponsored system of segregation in the realm of Jim Crow, that omission in the federal statutes was no small thing.

Although I was the only African American in the shop and was leading an all-white staff, I had never imagined that any of them harbored such hostile feelings about me. That was not to say, however, that I entertained any illusions about how some of them felt about my being their manager. Many a time I walked through the service department next door and not a single soul would open his mouth to acknowledge my existence. But seeing that picture was a shock. It jolted me into realizing that before I could go on with my work agenda, I had to massage the relationship with my crew. I knew that what I would say and do in that situation would determine how many of them would see me—and how they would see people who looked like me. My next move was critical.

Although they all were waiting on some demonstrative response, I did not say a word. Nor did I erase the ugly little sketch. As a matter of fact, I left it up for another three days. It was not that I did not know who did it. I knew each of their signature design styles and there was no question which fellow did it. It was Chris.

On the third day, while working on a screen print beside Chris, I turned to him. "Chris, why would you illustrate something as hideous as that?" I asked simply.

He was stunned. He tried to get himself together enough to come up with words of explanation. Of course, he had none. In response, I asked him to come into the office.

I am sure that Chris did not know what to expect as he stepped into my office. He probably thought I was going to berate him, throw him out of the office, and probably fire him. But that was not what I did.

Instead, I complimented Chris on his drawing technique, perspective, and dimension. Then I said, "The only problem, Chris, is that it is too small. I want you to erase it and draw it bigger. Fill up the whole board. Maybe I do need to be reminded of that."

Chris, of course, was flabbergasted.

"I ain't going to redraw that shit bigger," he declared.

At that point, I have to admit that I found it interesting that even he thought it was shitworthy. But I did not let that distract me.

"Chris, you can either draw it again or we can discuss it with the company president," I said.

In response, Chris gritted his teeth and grimly drew out the same image. This time, however, it spanned the entire board. When he was done, I let him leave my office. And I kept his drawing on the memo board for the rest of the day. And the day after that as well.

In fact, I kept that drawing up there for nearly two weeks.

Every day, Chris had to pass by my office where his handiwork stood in evidence. And he was not the only one. Visitors to the shop would come by, clearly take notice of the drawing, and nevertheless depart without saying a word. The tension and the shame were clearly tearing Chris up inside.

Finally, Chris came to me. He was nearly in tears. He pleaded that I allow him to erase it. He tried to explain the reasons for his action, telling me about a home in which his father had spewed racism rhetoric each night across the family's dinner table. He spoke of the election of Mayor Richard Arrington as the first black mayor of Birmingham in 1979. "Now there's a black man running this city," he said, in a sad mixture of confusion, betrayal, and contempt. Clearly Chris's world had shifted under his feet and the result was a sickening vertigo of emotion.

Shortly thereafter, I allowed Chris to remove the drawing. Needless to say, he was very grateful, and not long after that I actually heard from his mother. She wanted to meet me and asked that I come to the elementary school where she worked in the lunchroom. I did and found her to be one of the nicest, most pleasant people I could have hoped to meet. After that initial encounter, she invited me and my wife to her home. It was the first time a black person had been invited to their home for dinner, Chris told me. Naturally, I thought of a similar gesture years ago from Miss Nichols.

I accepted Chris's mother's invitation and, when my wife and I arrived, we all shouldered our way through the awkward initial pleasantries. But Chris's mother asked me to give thanks over dinner, and in the end it was a perfectly fine evening. In fact, a friendship between our families budded and blossomed. Chris's mother hand-stitched a christening outfit for my newborn son, Dale, and Chris's father even hand-carved a beautiful wooden crib for him. I still wonder what it must have taken for Chris's father to craft that crib.

When I think back on my experience with Chris and his family, I marvel at how an entire family was saved from themselves. After that encounter, it would be nearly impossible for them to see African Americans as they did before. Eventually, Chris's parents would introduce me as their "son." When Chris's father died, I went to the funeral. His mother hugged me so tightly that I did not think she would ever let me go.

None of this, however, is to say that I was not impacted by seeing that horrific image on that memo board. Even today, as I recreated that picture and mentally exhumed that moment in the process of telling this story and writing these pages, I became overcome by a great sense of hurt and shame. I became woefully aware of my people, some perhaps in my own lineage, who in fact were hung from tree limbs.

Halfway into recreating the drawing, I felt compelled to call my son. For ten minutes I just needed to unwind. We reflected on our journey and the wins and losses that had occurred. I looked across my art studio and at the matted and framed photo of the board of directors for Coca-Cola Bottling Company United, Inc. In that picture, I was one of *them*. It gave me strength and motivation to complete the drawing in reflection of the thirty-eight year relationship I have had with this remarkable brand, that remarkable family, and a teachable moment that ended well.

So often, when I share the story of Chris and that drawing, people remark on how saintly it was for me to not fire Chris on the spot. I suppose that would have been the easy thing to do. It would have been what most people would have done. But sometimes we need to do something out of the ordinary. We need to do something, from time to time, that causes people to ask, "Why did you do that?" Because if we do not, we risk not pausing to assess what we are doing. We risk simply going with the flow.

Think about Miss Nichols. Strictly speaking, her only job was to teach us about sentence fragments, nouns, verbs, adjectives, and how to pronounce the word "often" ("off-en"). Instead, she accomplished much, much more. She went well out of her way to make a difference in my life. And by doing so, she made a difference in the lives of countless others through me. I think our lives are far more fruitful when we go out of our way for the better good of a situation, other people, our community, and life in general.

To my nephew, I would say: People will listen to your actions far more carefully than they will your words. Your actions will reflect the significance or insignificance of your words. Some of the most pointed messages that you will ever communicate will occur without the employment of a single word. Let your actions, gestures, and deeds speak clearly. And remember—whoever said "those who deserve love the least, need love the most" certainly knew what he or she was talking about.

10

KNOW WHO YOU ARE

It is my opinion that far too many people are born, live, and die without ever actually gaining a genuine and inherent sense of self and purpose. Knowing who you are puts you in an incredibly comforting place. The confidence you gain makes taking firm positions an easier task. Knowing one's purpose gives one the courage to be moved or shaken only rarely by what others think. I also believe that a strong self-awareness breeds a sense of the importance of giving an extra measure of service.

In my mind, the one-and-only Howard Cosell embodied such a sense of self-awareness. Younger readers may not even know who Howard Cosell was. But to my generation, the legendary sportscaster, with his emphatically staccato voice and blustery personality, single-handedly occupied a place in the world of sports that today takes all of ESPN and a score of sports talk radio shows to fill.

Cosell died twenty years ago. In the wake of his passing, I remember watching a documentary about him. One story recounted in the film reminded me of how Cosell completely embodied not only cocksureness but a realization of how his talents could be brought to bear for a greater good.

As told by the documentary, Cosell left dinner one night in Kansas City with his friend and fellow sportscaster Al Richards. The men were headed to their destination in a big, white limousine. Their route led them through a rough neighborhood. At the stop light, they looked over and saw a brutal street brawl, surrounded by onlookers egging on the two combatants.

Cosell, dressed in a flashy yellow jacket with a cigar dangling from his mouth, hopped out of the limo and, without missing a beat, began to call the fight. Typically, of course, Cosell narrated the matches of the greatest athletes of all time—Muhammad Ali, George Foreman, and the like. But here he was, standing on a Kansas City street corner giving a blow-by-blow account of a street fight waged by two anonymous kids.

Somewhere between their blows, the young combatants noticed Cosell. Dropping their tired arms to their sides, they stood and marveled at the miraculous appearance of a man they had only seen on television.

Years later, Michaels recalled Cosell's words to the two bloodied fighters:

"*Now listen, it's quite apparent to this trained observer that the young southpaw does not have a jab requisite for the continuation of this fray. Furthermore, his opponent is a man of inferior and diminishing skills. This confrontation is halted posthaste!*"

Cosell did not know those guys. Nor did he know the circumstances of their disagreement. Nevertheless, he used his talents to diffuse the situation. When asked why he, a legend, stepped unbidden into such a situation, Cosell had a simple response: "I know who I am."

I never forgot that story because it speaks volumes. Standing on that street corner did not make Cosell less of a legend. He had a revelation that his gift, *in that moment*, could be used to make *that community* a better place. If he had not stopped to "call" that fight—if he had chosen to pass on by—who is to say what the outcome might have been.

Unlike Cosell, many people live and die and never figure out who they are. What a pity if they do not. It is just another reason to remember the "Miss Nichols Effect." Like Howard Cosell, she knew who she was. And she knew that many would consider it scandalous for her white family to invite a young, black man into their home for lunch. But she knew who she was and for what purpose she lived. She wasn't just a teacher, defined by an expected role of simply explaining the rules of grammar to the students who cycled through her classroom each year. Instead, she was a motivational coach who lived to inspire children. Imagine if she had just written me off and failed to speak words of life, living, and encouragement to me that day. I might have met a very different end. I shudder at the thought.

When you know who you are, what people do or attempt to do will not change that reality. Those who seek to diminish your character or misrepresent your cause will find that their efforts are futile. Remember—such was Chris's experience.

Many other circumstances and events tested my awareness of self during those earlier years at Coca-Cola. Those were days in which I was in the unique position of being a new manager, with all that that entailed, while also trying to prove my humanity to my staff and my immediate bosses. Both subordinates and superiors were white men who had been raised in the Jim Crow South to question me for no other reason than my hair texture and skin pigment. If I was not firmly grounded in my sense of self, what could I expect of them?

I remember a time when one particular gentleman who worked in our service department came to work so excited that he could not contain himself. John had just bought his wife a metallic green Cadillac with a white top and whitewall tires. He stopped everyone who crossed his path that morning to tell them about it in great detail—except me. That was not unusual; John never spoke to me. As a matter of fact, whenever I would come nearby, he would turn his back. And this particular morning, even with all of John's excitement, was no exception.

Later that day, I found myself in conversation with Steve, a member of my staff. Steve commented on John's new purchase and his obvious pride in it, but then shared with me some words he had exchanged with John a few months earlier.

"How does that nigger treat y'all over there?" John had asked Steve.

"First of all, he's not a nigger," Steve had replied. "And, second, I think he is a fine boss."

I appreciated what Steve was telling me but I did not necessarily believe him. "Come on," Steve, I said. "You can level with me. What did you really say?"

"I ain't kidding you, man. I hate that kind of shit."

That was typical Steve. And thank goodness for him. He was often a leveler for so many of these racial episodes during those days, which were far too many to mention. And let me hasten to say that this was not a problem unique to Coca-Cola, and it certainly was not cultivated by Coca-Cola's leadership. Sadly, it was simply part of Birmingham's still-evolving society in the 1970s.

But that did not make John's visceral racism any easier for me to stomach, and I was determined to erode John's baseless stance toward me and others like me. And, believe it or not, I also wanted to help him celebrate his special moment.

And so, under the shadow of his daily coldness, I worked to prepare a matching metallic-green, hand-lettered license nameplate for his wife. I took great pride in creating it, making sure it was the exact color of the new Cadillac. Steve helped me make sure the spelling of John's wife's name was correct, and I emblazoned it across the plate's front.

When I was done, I walked over and presented it to John.

"I noticed the beautiful Caddy for your wife," I told him. "I thought she might like having a personalized nameplate for it. I love making these for a few of my friends."

My kindness struck at John's core. It simultaneously arrested his ill will and, with a gesture of thoughtfulness, melted away all the hate and fear he harbored toward me. From that day forward, not only did John speak to me, but he regularly expressed his gratitude, often walking to my department just to say hello and to recount his wife's appreciation.

You may be asking yourself—why would I do that? Sometimes I wonder myself, but I believe that I have been endowed with a temperament and fortitude to see beyond momentary situations. I count that as a wonderful and worthwhile gift. We should use our gifts wisely.

Happily, at Coca-Cola in those days I had white colleagues and superiors who also seemed to be able to see beyond both the past and the challenges of the present. I spoke earlier of Coca-Cola's leadership and what appeared to be its firm position on leaving behind much of the old order's way of thinking and shouldering its responsibility as a transition agent.

For example, I remember going to visit a major grocer and significant Coca-Cola customer in the Bessemer community. My assignment, as detailed by our sales department, was to communicate to the customer what Coca-Cola could, and could not, provide in the way of signage for his location. About three sentences into my missive, the grocery's manager interrupted me with a flash of irritation.

"Boy, you don't tell me what I can and cannot have," he snapped. "You just go back and tell your bossman what I want."

Well, I thought, this will be interesting . . .

I returned to the Coca-Cola plant and shared my experience with our company president. With bated breath, I anticipated his response. And without delay, without missing a beat, and right in my presence and hearing, he called the manager of that grocery store. They first exchanged a few conversational pleasantries. Then he proceeded with what truly made me so proud to be a part of the Coca-Cola brand.

"Larry Thornton is our advertising manager," the president said, "and I understand that he has been out to see you. I'm going to ask him to come back to visit with you again . . . and to let you know what signage we can provide for your store." With that said, he hung up the phone.

"Now let's see how it goes this time," he said to me. And that was it. Validated in that manner, you can imagine just how very tall I felt. I probably lowered my head so as to not injure myself as I exited the doorway of his office.

Nevertheless, I was a bit uncertain of what to expect back in Bessemer. But I immediately headed back to the grocery store, thinking that my return visit to see this gentleman needed to follow as closely as possible his conversation with our company president. And sure enough, as I recall, it was an amiable, albeit somewhat passive, visit. I delivered on my assignment without incident or any fallout . . . or none that I was ever aware of. All I knew for sure was that my boss had forged a path for me back to Bessemer—and seemingly broadened the grocer's perspective in the process.

As for me, my cause is likewise to forge a path for those who look like me and to enlighten those who do not look like me. I often reflect on my ancestors of some fifteen to twenty generations past. I get my temperament from them. They were often faced with decisions that could affect not only themselves but generations to follow. I think about the slave who had to watch as his daughter or wife was taken and used and abused at will without recourse. He had to face the decision of whether to avenge her of these assaults and be killed with honor, or to grit his teeth, endure the unspeakable, and, at the end of the day, still be alive by his loved one's side to tend her wounds.

It is my opinion that, to the extent humanly possible, it is better to do the latter. Think about it. If the father or husband is killed, then you have killed the seed. And where does that leave that particular family tree?

For that reason, I am grateful for the Mr. Thorntons of generations past who possessed the necessary grit, fortitude, and forbearance to ensure that our family's seed was preserved. Perhaps even in their moments of greatest pain they took solace in hoping that their resilience might one day produce an Arthur Shores, Helen Shores Lee, A. G. Gaston, Rosa Parks, Fred

Legacy of Courage

ROSA PARKS

BUS RIDE • MONTGOMERY STREET SIGN • ROSA PARKS MUSEUM

Shuttlesworth, or even Larry Thornton, who would in their own time make small contributions to taming a Jim Crow South and righting injustices on an even broader sweep of history.

Remember my thinking from earlier. If you can't take anything, you can't have anything. Enduring the antics of my colleagues was nothing compared to what so many of my ancestors faced. Surely, I thought, I can be the bigger man in these situations. And the funny thing was that, in being the bigger man, I helped them to become bigger men themselves. Through me, they had an unexpected but incredibly meaningful experience with a single black man that, as it played forward, could possibly augment the way they see all men.

I am a believer that other people, both the Johns and the Steves of this world, will virtually lift you up and bring you to the desires of your heart. Your success is contingent upon the success of others. That is why I will continue my efforts to create an environment where people can thrive and grow—not just in relation to their job, but as men and citizens who seek to reverse any lingering grip and influence of the Jim Crow South in which I grew up.

To my great-great-granddaughter, yet unborn, I would say: first, how very dear you are to me and that I love you very much. What's your name? I would want you to understand that creative efforts for making this world better are far more fruitful than exploring efforts for getting even.

11

AN UNEXPECTED PHONE CALL

In 1988, I faced the daily challenge of simultaneously growing my de-partment while undertaking the necessary pruning of some of the men within it. At the same time, the soft drink industry in Alabama was facing its own challenges. Foremost among them was the state's threat to levy a highly unfavorable tax on beverages like Coca-Cola.

Fortunately, down in Montgomery, the legislature's Black Caucus was holding up the decision on the bill.

"Larry," the Coca-Cola president said, "we need you to go with us tomorrow morning to Montgomery. Pack some clothes."

Now this was a big deal for me. I was being commissioned by our company's president to go to the state capitol to help lobby against this tax. And I could barely spell "lobby," much less explain the process of what passed or defeated a bill.

Well, if he doesn't have any better sense than to ask me, a sign painter, to go and lobby for our company, I thought to myself, *then why should I have any better sense than to say anything other than "Yes, sir. I'll be ready"?*

And that was what I said—even though the task ahead of me was, to say the least, intimidating.

The next day, dressed and packed for the trip to Montgomery, I crowded into the company car with Eddie for the ninety-minute drive. As we rode south, my fellow co-workers and I discussed our mission. We were to engage with the African American legislators and fully explain the bill's various problems to them.

On the surface, that sounded like a manageable job. But there was just one problem—I did not know any of those legislators and certainly none of them knew me.

Nevertheless, once in Montgomery, I soon found myself sitting in one-on-one visits with lawmakers like Fred Horn, Earl Hilliard, and John Rogers. We met, talked, met again, and talked some more. And in the end the tax bill was defeated. Looking back on the effort, I think that, through simply showing up and expressing a genuine attitude of concern, we helped prevent the bill's passage and the unintended harm that it would have caused to our company and its constituents.

Riding back to Birmingham, I reflected on the experience. For me, it had truly been mind-blowing. I had just worked—successfully—on behalf of my entire organization in a critical statewide effort. I had come a long way from just being a sign painter with no greater ambition than to learn how to paint signs and leave as soon as I could.

Back home, I continued to think about my work in Montgomery, as well as the challenge that Coca-Cola had faced in the capitol. This spur-of-the-moment trip had revealed to me that there was a relationship void between Coca-Cola and the African American leadership in both the state legislature and in the larger Birmingham community. And to me that presented an opportunity. Someone, I thought, should make it a priority to get to know anyone and everyone in black leadership in the Birmingham area—the mayor's office, local colleges, the NAACP, the United Negro College Fund, and the Urban League, as well as any state, city, and county offices in our sales market.

I approached my colleague Eddie with the bold idea that that "someone" should be us.

"No way, man," Eddie responded. "They ain't going to pay you for that."

They ain't gonna pay me for that. I can't think of anything that will retard the growth and development of an individual more than the long-term adoption of this mindset.

The reality was that I really didn't need Eddie's buy-in of my idea as much as I needed access to his company car. Sadly, it should have been Eddie's idea in the first place. In addition to his company car, he already came to work in a shirt and a tie, with a wallet full of business cards that referenced him as a "market manager." It was a perfect setup for Eddie, but like so many, he just could not see the opportunity before him.

"I'm going to do it anyway, Eddie," I told him. "I just can't imagine the company not appreciating that."

"Well, don't get yourself in trouble because ain't nobody told us to be doing that," Eddie replied.

Admittedly, Eddie's reply gave me pause, because he was right—no one had told us to do such a thing. Perhaps that was understandable. I would have been the most unlikely candidate to be doing such a thing. I came to work in clothing fit for a sign painter. I drove a paint-soiled pickup truck. And I did not possess a single business card . . . at the time.

Nevertheless, seeking neither blessing nor permission from my boss, I set out on my mission to familiarize myself with Birmingham's leadership. I prepared a drawing of Dr. Martin L. King Jr. and placed it into production so that I could present framed prints on behalf of Birmingham Coca-Cola where appropriate. I looked for opportunities to provide Coca-Cola banners and cases of soft drinks at choice programs in the various legislative districts. I would bring a suit and tie to my paint shop, change clothes in my office, drive my shop pickup truck to various events—and park around the corner—to meet with state and local leaders.

After three or four months of having met more than twenty legislators, college presidents, and civic community leaders, I felt ready to share

my experiences with Claude Nielsen, our company president. But Eddie's words tormented my thoughts as I readied myself and my report. I was about to put my confidence to the test. I hoped I was right and Eddie was wrong because, if there was one thing upon which we could both agree, "ain't nobody" had asked me to do this.

The next day, I spent fifteen minutes overviewing my one hundred and twenty days of engagements with the president, all while simultaneously trying to get a read on his pending response.

When I finished, the president asked his first question. "Larry, how did you take these individuals to breakfast, lunch, and dinner? Who paid for the meals?"

"I did," I replied.

"With your own money?"

"Yes, sir."

The president then told me two things. First, he said how much he appreciated my efforts on behalf of the company. Second, he told me to complete an expense report so that I could be reimbursed for what I had spent on meals. It was no small sign of my inexperience in such work that up to that point I had never even heard of an expense report!

I was soon doing as much community and public relations work for Coca-Cola as I was sign painting. The business cards came first. Then came the company vehicle with a car phone. Before long, completing expense reports became commonplace. I had reinvented myself and was well on my way to designing a very different Larry Thornton. Meanwhile, Eddie was scratching his head and trying to process how I had transitioned from the sign shop to relationship management.

Without even realizing it, Eddie and I were striking our own bargains with life. Through what I would call a flawed attitude of approach, Eddie was promulgating a self-inflicted wound to his own growth and development.

Neither of us necessarily realized it at the time, but Eddie was working for the company, and I, on the other hand, was working for life.

I had not kept tabs on the hours I spent catching up on the signs that were due. Nor had I sought overtime for the late nights and weekends I spent trying to hit the targeted requests to meet the sales department's demands. I never asked for commission fees for my Martin Luther King Jr. drawing, which would become one of the most popular images of him in and around Birmingham. I was not tallying, in those days before DVR, the sporting events and TV programs I missed. I was not keeping tabs of the meals that I paid for at many of those leadership breakfasts and lunches and dinner. But life surely was.

I often wonder what Eddie would think today, to know that the same corporation that he thought wouldn't pay us for a little extra effort now pays me, as a board member, more for about fifteen hours of sharing my thoughts, asking a few questions, and making or seconding a motion, than he or I earned in a year. And that, in fact, three corporations have paid me consistently for more than twenty-five years to serve at the highest executive levels.

To my nephew I would say: Put the time in, make the investment of your best effort and your best thinking. Do your best, mean your best to everyone that you frequent. That is what it means to give your best. "Work for life" so that life can work for you!

12

THE PAY-OFF ISN'T ALWAYS MONEY

Over the years, I have discovered that life rewards us for our service. It should not be measured only in dollars and cents. It's one thing to make a dollar . . . it's quite another thing to make a difference!

Some people might envy their perception of my financial wherewithal, I suppose, but I am far prouder of the myriad opportunities life has afforded me to serve others in roles such as being a board member at the Alabama Institute of Deaf and Blind and the Community Foundation of Greater Birmingham. These appointments position me to encourage and motivate and to enrich others in my community. I am convinced that I exist for that very purpose and I take the greatest measure of pride and joy in trying my best to not miss a single opportunity for doing so.

One of the ways I am rewarded is with the opportunity to work with my son in our business every day. He is by far the finest son that any father could ever expect to have. And for those of you who might think that I am saying that because he is my son, you are absolutely right! To celebrate with the employees and customers I love and respect who have been a part of my organization fifteen, twenty, and even twenty-five years as we celebrate our twenty-fifth year in business.

There are those who do not think service to others has value. To them, money and riches is what they seek. There are many sterling examples of such thinking—the man who is always looking for something for nothing, the woman hopping in and out of local casinos, the family hoping for the genie to appear, the teenager waiting for his proverbial ship to come in.

But in truth, if you did not send a ship out, there is a pretty good chance that there will not be a ship coming in . . . at least not one for you.

But if a ship full of cash *does* arrive at your dock, I have some cautionary advice for you—I have found money to be one of the dumbest things you could ever put your hands on. It offers no suggestion or opposition to its use, whether it is being used wisely or unwisely. It will not defend itself if being abused, nor will it offer any ideas or encouragement on making better use of itself. It is not committed or dedicated to anyone. It is typically one of the most willing participants in a financial transaction, while taking no responsibility for the success or failure thereof. It will not rejoice with you when used resourcefully, nor will it share in your remorse when used poorly. In short, money just does not care—which means it is entirely up to you as to how to handle it. Handle it wisely or handle it foolishly. Either way, it is up to you. But know this: in hands controlled by an unprepared mind (whether they be the hands of your children, family, loved ones, or otherwise), the use of money will almost always prove futile.

Earn New Rules

In life, you have to have rules. And generally people do not like rules. But if you do not have rules, then you will have chaos. Happily, if you do not like the rules to which you are subjected, you can earn a new set. When you become a person who proves that you can operate above average, you'll likely graduate to a new set of rules and leave the old, more restrictive ones behind.

For example, I soon reached a point in my career at Coca-Cola in which I was driving a company car to facilitate business. Meanwhile, there was a company rule that you could not drive outside of our sales territory. As the advertising manager for Birmingham, I would go about the city and do my job, but I would occasionally drive to Montgomery because of my connections there in helping Coca-Cola build relationships.

Richard, the fleet manager, noticed that I obviously was racking up more miles than would be customary for driving within our sales market. With a misplaced sense of satisfaction at catching me in some wrongdoing, he reported me to our president.

"Your colleagues are watching you," the president said to me over the car phone—and then laughed about it.

Richard didn't know that rule did not apply to me. He was so busy trying to find a bug in my soup that he failed to make sure his own bowl was bug-free. Richard was seemingly well-versed in the rules about company car usage. He was apparently less familiar—or less concerned about—the rules against sleeping on the job. Often one could find Richard tucked around the corner in his office, sound asleep and snoring like an ox. On one such occasion, I used my Polaroid camera to snap a few candid shots of him in his slumbering glory. And, after my call from our company president, I paid Richard a visit.

"Your colleagues are watching you," I said, as I slipped the photos onto his desk. "You might want to be careful."

But I never said a word about Richard's sleep habits to the president. My mama often told me that if you find yourself digging a ditch for people, you better dig two—one for them and one for you. I suspect that on that day Richard had learned that lesson, too.

I would say to my granddaughter: Put yourself in the way of what's happening on the job, in the church, in your community, and in your home. Fill the obvious void, in addition to your current sphere of responsibilities. How else can you demonstrate the added value that you bring in these areas? In so many instances, the idea of waiting to be told by the boss to carry out what is clearly a sterling opportunity is silly, non-productive, and serves as the primary culprit for too many missed opportunities to number.

13

DESIGN YOUR OWN PAST

As my early years passed at Coca-Cola, I became more and more amazed at the successes I was achieving with the company. It was hard for me to imagine me, the underperforming boy from Madison Park, climbing the ranks of a major corporation. Had I known in those Madison Park days what I came to know at Coca-Cola, my thinking and my attitude would have been much different a long time ago.

Imagine for a moment the value any of us might have added to our present-day quality of life if we had acted upon a certain decision ten years earlier. Or, what if we had gripped an opportunity that was available just five years ago, or capitalized on a plan just a year or two ago? Now this is not the time to fall into regret or despair about lost opportunities. Rather, let those questions motivate us to maximize future opportunities so that we will not again have cause to look back with regret.

After being let go from Vestavia Hills High School, I decided to create for myself a master class in life and living. I read books, studied vocabulary words, and memorized motivational quotes. I took to heart the Jim Rohn admonition: "Work harder on yourself than on any job." I was working for life and I wanted to make sure that I was the top employee. The more I learned, the more confident I became that I could really approach life with a goal to win at it.

During this time, I read a quote by Winston Churchill. The former

British prime minister once said, "History will be kind to me . . . for I intend to write it." I suppose you could interpret Churchill as meaning that, with him writing the story of his own life and times, he would paint himself in the most flattering light. But I interpreted his words differently. I think he meant that he intended to take charge of his own history and write it as it was happening. And that's what my self-taught master class encouraged me to do. I was going to work at designing my own past as it was unfolding.

"Designing our past." Think about that idea. It may seem counterintuitive. After all, the past is the only written-in-stone aspect of our lives. But if that is indeed the case, then we want to be happy when, in the future, we look back on it. So how do we get to that point?

That's what I mean by designing our past. We need to think—now—about who we want to be in the future and put in the work—now—so that this past we are creating—now—will be the launching pad for the future at which we are aiming. Why not, then, work hard, plan smart, and creatively design our efforts to make memories pleasant? In other words, work hard in the present to make the future easy.

One thing is for certain: we cannot change, undo, or recreate historical events. It is a fact that, in many instances, our past personal management missteps, poor decision-making skills, unwarranted emotional strains, and misplaced anger haunt us. The result is an intangible yet insidious gravitational-like pull on our lives.

But do not despair. A Turkish proverb states that it doesn't matter how far down the wrong road you've gone, it is never too late to turn back. We absolutely cannot afford to miss this very basic and primordial principle of positive change.

Imagine if we were to take full advantage of one of our most prized assets—our power to choose. Decide today on moments of your past, as you would have them appear. You are capable of knowing today the quality of life you wish to enjoy ten years from now. Act on that! You can also know today the opportunities you wish to take advantage of over the next five years and capitalize today on plans and ideas you might set into motion, monitoring closely their execution over the next two years, one year, or even the next six months. Do it!

What Are You Thinking?

As you can understand, the challenge of writing one's life story requires vision—sometimes beyond our natural ability to see or touch, but vision that is intuitive according to our thinking. We best initiate this new path of designing our past, I think, by taking serious inventory of our thinking. Take an honest and straightforward assessment of your values and philosophies. Would you believe that we are, for the most part, nothing more than a product of the sum total of our yesterdays and our collective past experiences? These experiences have refined our thinking, our philosophy of thoughts, and beliefs.

If such is the case, then the fundamental question becomes: What have my thoughts produced? What about this present day me? More importantly, what kind of past will I design over the next five years if I continue my current mode of thinking?

I almost fell into the trap of poor thinking. Growing up convinced of my inferiority, I could have accepted that status and greeted what that experience would have had for me. That gentleman who came into the Majik Mart each day when I was a teen was convinced he was not going to be anything and I had agreed with him that I, too, was headed that way. Thank goodness that I amended my thoughts.

If you are comfortable with where and what your thinking has brought you, then by all means continue to cultivate and even accelerate your current pattern of thinking. If you don't relish your current position, then give yourself permission to abort that paradigm of thought. Don't be resigned to that old tiresome cliché, "That's just the way I am." Instead, realize that the way that you are is not the way that you have to be.

For the first dozen or so years of my career, art and art-related interests had permeated my thinking. Any thoughts or potential opportunities outside of the artistic arena were always considered off limits. I dismissed them without even a casual consideration. "I am an artist," I would always tell myself.

But thinking of myself as an artist was, after all, just how I thought. I did not realize that how I thought was not necessarily the way that I *had to* think. Was it possible, just maybe, for me to satisfy my cravings for traditional business interest and still maintain my interest in art?

Well, it is now twenty-five years later. I have owned and operated six restaurants. The answer is clear—my business and creative sides can coexist and quite often work in wonderful unison. Consider the fact that I completed my most prized piece of art, an original oil-pencil rendition of legendary poet Maya Angelou (see next page). I even had the awesome opportunity to present the first print of the series to Dr. Angelou in a public ceremony.

Upon receiving my work, Dr. Angelou asked if I could make a print for her friend. "Yes, of course," I said. "Who might that be?"

"Oprah Winfrey," she replied.

This limited edition series clearly represented a hallmark moment in my artistic career, right in the midst of my business career. What a pity it would have been if I had given up my art entirely to start an unrelated business. But there's the point: it's all related! We are not one-dimensional beings. I am now more convinced than ever that my thinking plays a critical role in my quest for self-actualization. I am limited or enlarged by what I think.

Damaging Thought Patterns

Consider how often we buy into mundane yet damaging thought

patterns that contribute immensely to a not-so-proud past. Here are my top ten most-damaging thought philosophies as they relate to winning in life.

- What's going to happen is going to happen anyway.
- I don't care (what others think of me).
- I've gone too far/long to change now.
- I'm not going in early or working one minute more than I'm paid. What's in it for me?
- I'm too old to do that.
- I was born poor and I'll die poor.
- I can't do it. It's too hard.
- I've tried once. I'm not trying again.
- If it's for me it'll come, God willing. (I happen to believe that God is always willing.)
- Leave me alone. (Alone is a dangerous and treacherous place to be left.)

Our thinking is paramount to the artful design of our new past. Get excited. Be optimistic about a new opportunity for what could be a part of our past. Make concrete decisions now. Do not settle for some capricious notion toward change, but rather steadfastly adhere to a fixed new direction that is grounded in the rudiments of personal discipline.

Change really is good. In fact, change is necessary to a more wholesome and complete life. Engaging and embracing progressive change invigorates the mind at any stage of life. It is always nice to watch those who are settling in and preparing their retreat from the push and pull of life. But it is extraordinarily exciting to watch those at any stage of life who are passionately anticipating the next challenge. That spirit represents the very essence of life. I think that it further differentiates "living life" from "just being alive."

I believe, with every fiber of my being, that, like a conductor who injects himself or herself into the direction of the melodious and instrumental harmony of a well-orchestrated musical score, or the creative and painstaking positioning of brushstrokes upon the canvas of an artist's masterpiece, we can indeed design our past.

Now, designing a past that we will be proud of and willing to hold in high esteem, and one that is representative of our truest self-image, will not happen by chance or luck. Rather, changes will come as a result of purposeful thought, planning and hard work. Thomas Jefferson said, "My good luck has always been in direct proportion to my hard work. The harder I work, the luckier I am." He makes an interesting and true point.

To my aunt, I would say: When we are finally comfortable with forgiving and then dismissing the mayhem of our yesterdays, and are ready to challenge our own reticence, we are then best positioned to confront change as a welcomed and natural part of what we've come to know as this process of humanity. Now let the sweet commencement of winning and designing our past begin.

14

OUR SIXTEEN HOURS

If you've read this far into my book, you might be thinking, "Well, that all sounds great, Larry, but I barely have enough time in my day for what I *have* to do. You talk about serving my community and designing my future and a lot of other things. I don't have time for that!"

Time can be one of our most illusory possessions. We all at various moments tend to think we have more or less time than we do. Naturally, therefore, we tend to abuse time, or fail to capitalize on it, without even realizing what we are doing. The mindset of *thinking that we have more time* than we actually do, often leads to procrastination and costly delays. The mindset of *thinking that we don't have enough time* can cause us to eliminate and/or omit worthwhile and rewarding projects. I have discovered that mastering our time can change our whole world. If I could pick a single most important lesson that I would share with my family, it would be the discipline of time well-spent. After all, if we really thought about it, not much would take greater precedence or have greater significance than our time.

While there are twenty-four hours in a day, there are significantly fewer hours during which we can truly be productive. The average amount of time we have for productivity, after subtracting a much-needed eight hours of rest, is about sixteen hours. When I learned to become a better steward of those sixteen hours, my whole world changed. With that in mind, I invite you to consider what I think of as seven principles of effective time stewardship.

Seek Balance

With only sixteen hours to utilize in a day, balance is essential. Creating and nourishing a body that thinks and functions properly requires rest, but spending too much time resting at the expense of activity or too much activity at the expense of rest is almost always self-defeating. In all things we must find BALANCE. Learning to respect the inseparable relationship between rest and activity aids in our ability to see more clearly why our sixteen hours are an extremely valuable asset.

We all could do a better job of extracting more from our sixteen hours—claiming more of a return from the hours that we spend with employment; more from the hours that we spend with our family and friends; more from our playtime and leisure time, our spiritual, personal and professional development, health and wellness, our downtime, reflection time; and perhaps even more from the time we spend in support of others.

Doing so, however, is easier said than done. So many of us never seem to have enough time. Others, on the other hand, awe us as to how they do it all. These people—obviously engaged—always seem somewhat serene and unruffled, generally available, and unrushed. They even appear to anticipate *new* opportunities, which, naturally, will require even more of their finite time. So what secret deal did they cut with time? Do they know something that we don't?

The truth is that none of us enjoys preferential favor with time. We have all been dealt the same hand—twenty-four hours a day. And one day will render only about sixteen hours of activity. Our challenge, therefore, is to convert activity into productivity.

Don't Lose Track of Time

We tend to trivialize the idea of "losing track of time." We use this phrase frequently and frivolously in our daily experience. Sometimes we are completely unconscious of its larger and more profound relevance to our very lives.

Whether we refer to time spent with our families, time spent updating our wills, or time spent initiating the next phase of our financial plans, this "losing track of time" is the culprit that contributes most significantly to time abuse.

The fact is that when we consider just how little time we really have, it's easy to see that we quite literally have no time to lose. At some point, we have to ask the question: What am I going to do with this little time and this little energy that I am so privileged to have? This begs an even greater and more profound question: How can this little time and this little energy that we have possibly accommodate our vast and great desires?

Taking advantage of as many opportunities as possible to extend our personal, professional, and spiritual reach is essential. And, when we set out to create an environment that facilitates our reach to those around us, we inevitably spend time developing our own character. This approach constitutes a great start in accounting for our available time.

Seek to Invite Order

Much of the productivity we seek may be found simply by taking a more ordered approach to our available time. It is said that where there is order, there is little to do. Organizing our sixteen hours can create the appearance of more time much the same as the illusion of more space appears when we reduce clutter and organize our garage, our cabinets, drawers or luggage.

Several years ago, I found myself faced with the dilemma of a scheduled bank board meeting at which I was to make a presentation, as chairman of our audit committee, while I had a crucial McDonald's marketing conference call scheduled for the same time. After attending a portion of the meeting and making my report, I was allowed to take my conference call in the office of the bank chairman, Richard Anthony.

I was struck by how well-organized everything in Anthony's office appeared. I was particularly impressed with his desk and work area. How could the chairman, president and CEO—and one of the most unassuming individuals that I know—of a large banking system maintain a work area so organized? He must have hundreds of letters to read, documents to review, and contracts to sign. This caused me to visualize my own business and my own desk and work area at that time. I will admit that the contrast was humbling.

Wondering if Anthony's superior system of organization had somehow been quickly arranged to impress me, I found ways to visit his office at future board meetings. What I found was more of the same. It was as if no work went on there ever. But clearly it did, as was evident from our board discussions at every meeting.

Even with that example, I was still not quite convinced that I should alter my own approach to business and organization. Therefore, I thought I would consider the organizational habits of an example that was more consistently available to me. He was something of a mentor to me and a person who I thought epitomized business acumen: the chairman, president and CEO of the largest independent Coca-Cola bottler in the nation. Surely, the office that orchestrated the largest independent Coca-Cola bottler in the nation would bear all of the "busy" indicators of which I could identify. But I found no such thing. Instead, during visit after visit—announced and unannounced—I found impeccable consistency of order. I now had little choice but to rethink my own return on investment with regard to the time I spent at work.

Acting on such observations, I found numerous opportunities to immediately take a more ordered approach to letters and documents, emails, returning calls, scheduling, and various other daily business tasks. My new attitude was "handle it now" and "share the load." Before long, others were asking me, "How do *you* get it all done?"

With that, I continued paying attention to the desks and work areas of several other highly successful and highly effective individuals—not to be confused with simply very busy individuals. I found these individuals to be consistently very organized and very ordered in their approaches. They anticipated new assignments and were committed to greater results. Practically bursting with new ideas and intuitively looking for more simplified approaches, they almost always seemed to start each project with the end in mind, believing that this mindset would expedite the project and provide enough focus and clarity to dispel unwarranted interruptions or distractions. These highly successful people clearly understood the connection between order and time.

Incredible responsibility demands incredible order. For me, the lesson was clear. The more order you invite, the more time you'll have.

I had a recent conversation with a CEO about business and life. Somehow, our chat led to socks. The man shared with me that to make his morning routine more stress-free, he got rid of all of his colored socks and switched to all black ones. That way, in the mornings, he is not digging through his drawer looking for a blue or a tan or a striped sock to match his outfit. Black goes with everything. That may seem like a small, insignificant change, but when you think about how many times we've all been delayed in search of a matching sock, it makes perfect sense. When I heard his story, I was sold. I switched to all black socks, too.

Don't Be Late

I am an avid proponent of the power of unspoken messages. St. Francis of Assisi said, "Go forth and preach the gospel always . . . and, when necessary, use words." What a tremendous testimony to the strength of deeds and actions. Ironically, those messages can be even more powerful when they are unwarranted or unintended. Being habitually late, I think, sends an irrevocable message that voids the significance of just about any individual and/or their purpose. Plainly stated, when we're late, we lose—end of story. Whether late for an appointment, late on an assignment, late in acting on a new idea, or late in planning, we are more often than not too late to take advantage of opportunities.

Such concerns were front and center in my mind when, in 2003, I was elected to the board of directors of Coca-Cola Bottling Company United, Inc. This was the same company that hired me in 1979 as a five-dollar-an-hour sign painter. My election was, understandably, one of the highest honors of my career. When I think back to when the new chairman told me that he wanted me in the board seat formerly held by the man whose grandfather founded the company in 1902, words fail me. And this new chairman was the same man who, in 1992, had made a point of breaking away from his own incredibly busy schedule to be a participant at my first McDonald's groundbreaking. I also recall the attendance that day of the man whose seat I would one day take on the company's board of directors. To this day, I proudly display a photograph of the two of us, as well as the first two dollars that he spent commemorating the moment.

Suffice it to say that after fifteen years of service, I was not going to let him down. I have never missed or been late for a board meeting or a committee meeting. What an unmistakably clear and unspoken message to both the board and the board chairman of how much I appreciated the opportunity to serve at the highest executive levels of this great organization.

And that message was not overlooked. Within three years of being named to the board, the board selected me as chairman of its audit committee. I suspect I had successfully convinced everyone that I not only appreciated and valued being on the board in the first place, but that I appreciated and valued their time as well. I imagine that the chairman put a high value on his audit committee meetings starting on time and the committee reports being delivered on time.

Early in my career, a gentleman of great success and stature said to me that as much as eighty percent of my success would be contingent upon my showing up . . . AND SHOWING UP ON TIME, he added with emphasis. I never forgot those words of admonition. To be sure, whatever the appropriate percentages are, our ability to show up and to show up on time is paramount to a life of winning.

We're just too busy, too consumed—or so we *think*. We're just so pre-occupied, too involved—or so we *think*, with the mundane, ordinary and commonplace issues of life that we rarely get to that real area of self-actualization—that area that genuinely represents our truer image and innermost personal conviction. Developing a nonnegotiable appreciation and respect for time tends to create tremendous opportunities for personal growth. It really is a matter of time—and planning accordingly.

Robert Ford—"Mr. Ford," as we all call him—was the first employee I hired at McDonald's more than twenty-five years ago. He was in charge of restaurant maintenance for my organization and still stops by our restaurants occasionally to give us pointers. I was so proud that his family asked me to be the featured speaker for his ninetieth birthday party just last year. He was the only maintenance man whom I invited regularly to our manager meetings because he essentially always had something significant to say. And what he said about being on time was one of the most significant things he ever said. "In order to be on time," he said, "you have to leave on time. Whether I'm going to work, or visiting a church in Detroit, Michigan, I'm on time because I leave in time to be on time."

Mr. Ford's basic, yet essential, wisdom remains a major motivator for me to this day. I've grown to realize that, generally, we don't plan to be late. Instead, we fail in our planning to be on time.

Conserve Time

Few things bring me more pleasure than spending a slow Sunday afternoon preparing a large meal for the week. Both of my parents were terrific cooks; naturally, growing up around them I developed a rather sharp affinity for food. More often than not, this meal includes my world-famous (well, world-famous to my family) baked chicken while enjoying a great glass of wine. When I'm finished, I enjoy the fruits of my creation, preferably with family and friends. But before I put away the leftovers, I usually separately store three to four single-servings for future meals. I never gave this convenience and time-sensitive approach a second thought until a dinner guest inquired about my rationale. It didn't take me long to make my case. It just seemed like a better approach than removing all the food from the refrigerator each time I needed to reheat a single serving.

There must be hundreds of similar examples that illustrate time conservation—from packing to avoid baggage claim on short trips to putting certain things (like car keys) in specific places. Even putting things back where they belong, as simple as it sounds, is a great timesaver. Thinking and planning ahead probably represents the single most significant opportunity for making the most of our sixteen hours.

Don't Stop for Yield Signs

How frustrating it is to be driving behind someone who chooses to come to a complete stop at a yield sign. Perhaps the person is stopping out of fear, in the interest of safety (from their perspective), or just not paying attention. The same might be true in our own daily experiences. We will often bring our normal living to a complete standstill for the same reasons—for fear, in the interest of safety and security, or just not paying attention. We stop for what could be a simple yield.

Clearly, life presents situations that both demand and even deserve our complete and undivided attention. But maybe it isn't always necessary to stop completely when faced with a curve or obstacle on the road of life. Some circumstances might require only a respectful pause.

Who can determine for someone else whether one of life's challenges should merit a complete stop as opposed to a mere pause? It is an individual call. I think the challenge as we seek to become better stewards of our sixteen hours is to question those things that we stop for and simply ask, "How often am I stopping for yield signs?" and "Am I missing significant opportunities to get on with and improve my life?" It is not always an easy choice to stop or to yield, but it is a choice. It is, in fact, your choice!

"Stitch" Character

"A stitch in time saves nine," the old proverb says. But too often, rather than managing through "strength of character" on the front end, we spend too much time trying to stitch together and mend poor performance on the back end. This is one of the more consistently missed opportunities in business. Getting our managers to realize the benefits of getting the job done through personal demeanor, disposition, and deportment is, for whatever reason, a real challenge. I've always thought it was wise to protect and develop who you are by guarding what you joke about, what you allow yourself to laugh at, and what casual conversation you allow yourself to engage in. Enhancing our personal strength of character better positions us, I think, to command the performance and/or response we seek. We will spend less time, for instance, "whipping employees into shape" if we behave in ways that say to our subordinates (and our superiors, for that matter) what is acceptable and what is not. By exhibiting our strength of character, we automatically address issues that might otherwise require our time.

Work is the premier consumer of our sixteen hours in so many cases. We absolutely cannot afford to miss the added-value opportunities that most employment settings provide. So often we go to work, get our checks, claim our benefits, and feel that we have been reasonably compensated.

Too often we don't realize, recognize, or take advantage of the tremendous people opportunities, relationship opportunities, and personal growth opportunities that are left on the table. These unspecified benefits are usually ours for the asking. We can all learn by taking advantage of the exposures and educational wherewithal of others, travel experiences of others, and even life-altering experiences of others. Time does not allow us to read everything, go everywhere, or do all that we'd like to do. But by paying attention to lessons all around us, we may come closer to attaining our own goals without the expense or time investment it would take to learn in conventional settings.

So there you have it. Seek balance. Don't lose track of time. Seek to invite order. Don't be late. Conserve time. Don't stop for yield signs. Stitch character. Each of these principles recognizes the intrinsic value of time. Actualizing our personal, professional, and spiritual goals depends on it.

To my daughter, I would say: understand that time is one of your most valuable assets. Plan your time well, guard your time always, conserve and save your time wisely. Don't waste your time in your earnest efforts for designing a better path for yourself and others.

15

THE ROCKY ROAD TO FREEDOM

What would you do if you were not afraid? That is a question we all might ask ourselves. I had always wanted to own a traditional business, and, as the years passed at Coca-Cola, it became more obvious that the time to do so was nearing. Sure, I had experience managing our advertising department and managing my private sign accounts, but I felt a tug to venture out and do more.

As advertising manager of Coca-Cola, I was not comfortable with my pace in climbing the corporate ladder, even though the company was treating me more than fairly. I thought I had more to offer. After all, I was "working for life," not for Coca-Cola, and I discerned that life had decided to promote me to business owner.

Several years earlier, life had similarly promoted a friend of mine, Herman Petty. On December 21, 1968, Petty became the first African American to acquire a McDonald's franchise. When I visited his store in Chicago, I was struck by the number of white patrons he had. This world of McDonald's had not only opened up amazing experiences for his family, but also for the surrounding community. I was intrigued.

Petty talked to me about opportunities springing up in the South. I wondered if his success could be replicated in Birmingham. I admitted to him that I did not know anything about running a McDonald's; Petty, in turn, insisted that I should give it a shot. The more I thought about it, the idea of opening a McDonald's seemed like a natural progression for me. Coca-Cola and McDonald's had been partners since 1955. Marrying those brands made perfect sense.

Thanks to Herman, I was pre-vetted to enter the owner/operator program. His endorsement, coupled with my twelve years of service with Coca-Cola, got me in the door toward owning a McDonald's franchise.

It might surprise you—it certainly did me—to learn that the McDonald's owner-operator training program is an eighteen-month to two-year exercise. When I found out that I would be looking at as much as two years in training, I said, "You are kidding me? Does it take that long to learn to make a McDonald's hamburger?" After all, I already knew how to make a hamburger. Adjusting to meet the McDonald's specifications should not take two years.

But, of course, it was not that simple. Nor was it as mundane as merely cooking hamburgers. In fact, the training was rigorous. Lots of people thought they could run a McDonald's, but McDonald's was not looking for just anyone. McDonald's was looking for a special type of person. The company's leadership wanted to know if you had the juice. Were you willing to make a personal investment in the success of your franchise? Can you come in early and stay late? Can you master every task in the restaurant? Can you do it day after day? "Hamburger University," as McDonald's called its training program, was going to test my fortitude, but I thought I was up for the challenge, even though I would be doing so while holding down my full-time responsibilities at Coca-Cola.

Thirteen months later, I had succeeded and, upon my graduation from Hamburger University, I received my offer for my first restaurant. I made the decision to pursue a McDonald's store and put in my notice to resign at Coca-Cola. Coca-Cola's president did not accept my resignation, however. He asked if I could stay on and do both.

I was honored that Coca-Cola did not want me to leave, and I decided to accept my president's offer. However, I braced myself for what I knew would be an intense experience. Starting a restaurant was going to be tough enough; now I faced the additional challenge of juggling my time and responsibilities between my new ownership career and my ongoing work for Coca-Cola.

When we are faced with a challenge, like the one upon which I was preparing to embark, there is one thing that makes it either doable or impossible. That one thing is perspective.

Think about the number 16/32. That seems like one of those mind-boggling fractions that had me stumped in fourth-grade math class. But look at that number again. At the end of the day, 16/32 is only 1/2.

When we bear down and really see a situation for what it is, it is likely not nearly as difficult as it might seem. Look at it again and see how you can create a plan to make it manageable. Maybe your situation requires you to first get to 8/16. For other situations, it might be 4/8, or perhaps even 2/4. But, in every case, they all still equal 1/2.

Unfortunately, life tends to present itself to us from a 16/32 perspective. The trick is to reject that perspective and find the simpler, more straightforward perspective. Just about every situation can really be as simple as 1/2. Accordingly, let "I can do this" be your mantra. Think that you can, believe that you can, and it will come to pass. And remember what Henry Ford once said, "Whether you think you can or you think you cannot, you are right."

Training to run a restaurant while working at Coca-Cola and tending to my family had looked, at the time, to be a complicated 16/32 fraction. Fortunately, I had the gift of perspective. At the end of the day, 16/32 was still just 1/2. I just needed to take it one job, one sign, and even one hamburger at a time.

And so I embarked upon this journey. My days were long, starting with my getting up at three in the morning, carrying my full-time job responsibilities at Coca-Cola, and then putting in another twenty hours a week at McDonald's for no pay. Even though it was grueling, I thought it would yield results that were bigger than me. It wasn't about burgers and fries; it was about introducing entrepreneurship into my family legacy and providing jobs and resources for my community. Again I told myself, "If I can't take anything, I can't have anything." This excruciating effort was an investment not just for my future, but for that of a world of people I could not even imagine.

That's not to say, however, that I greeted every early morning or long night with a joyous heart. My daughter can attest to that. She often listened to me complain about the unceasing challenges that I seemed to be continually facing. Finally, however, she had heard enough.

"Daddy, you shouldn't complain about the fight," she said. "Just be thankful that you are up for the fight—and, besides, you fight so well!"

Wow, I thought. Did my daughter just say that? What a needed message to hear. What a profound message for us all.

There is a sports commercial that says, "What you do in the dark will put you in the light." I can testify to the truth of that axiom. I spent a lot of predawn mornings and late-night evenings working. Of course, I would have rather been in my warm bed or watching one of my favorite television programs, but I am a witness that the hard work no one sees eventually propels you to a stage where the fruits of your labor will be on public display.

Six other African American registered applicants in the Atlanta region began the McDonald's training with me. We had all been reasonably successful already. But this exercise would call for an extra measure of grit. Only two of us made it to the end: a woman named Sandra and myself. Sandra opened her McDonald's restaurant in Atlanta and after two and a half years, she exited the McDonald's system. In July 2017, I celebrated the twenty-fifth anniversary of the opening of my first restaurant. Of my class from the training program, I was literally the last man standing. *If you can't take anything, you can't have anything.* The more you can take, the more you can have for you, your family and your community.

But, when you try to pursue something out of the ordinary, there will be casualties. I have heard it said on several occasions—everyone that comes with you, cannot necessarily go on with you. That is painfully and uncomfortably true.

I met a guy years ago who went through the McDonald's training program and got all the way up to Hamburger University. He dropped out just shy of completing the program because his wife thought it was too much. Quite often, you might find those closest to you struggling to identify with you and your purpose, your calling, and your work.

I'm thinking that would be like my grandfather leaving the field in mid-July just before the harvest. What would it look like if he gave up after having already turned the ground in April through May, carefully fashioning each row for the corn, the peas, and the potatoes; having endured the painstaking exercise of planting the well-prepared seeds row after row after row; having returned to the field day after day to fight the weeds only to return the next week as the summer grew warmer to fight the same weeds, the same bugs, the heat, the rain, and the stench of the mule?

I can remember the many times that my grandmother would send me to find my grandfather in the field at midday to deliver a quart-sized canning jar of ice water and pork fat biscuits for his lunch. His quietly radiant jubilance would greet me. As a kid, I always thought his reaction had do with seeing his grandson. But as I reflect today, and remember his sweat-drenched overalls, I'd say his enthusiasm had much more to do with the ice water.

I wonder what my grandfather's response would have been if my grandmother had said to him, "Major, that's just too much. It's taking too long. You been going to that field day after day since April or May and you never come home with any corn. Now it's the middle of July, why don't you just quit that?" Would he have stopped going to the field? After all, rocking on that front porch listening to the radio or sitting under the shade of that huge chinaberry tree in the front yard might have been an attractive alternative to the bugs and heat of the field.

If my grandmother had ever raised such an idea, would my grandfather have even attempted to educate my grandmother on the rudiments, the disciplines, and the principles of farming?

Would she have listened?

I like to think that he might have said, with passion, "Julia, we are just days away now from fruition [not that my grandfather would have ever used such a word as fruition] from the harvest." In his own words, he might have explained why he had been chopping the weeds so that they would not take the earth's nutrients that were intended for the corn, and going back to the field to fight the bugs that would destroy the crop, and ignoring the heat of an Alabama summer day. He might have explained that, even though there was no corn yet to bring home, the daily evidence was already suggesting that in the fall they would reap a bountiful return.

"Julia Mae, just listen to me," he might have said. "Hear me now. We are so close. The one kernel of corn that we invested in the earth, in just a few more days will yield for us three to four ears of corn—each ear bearing as many as six hundred kernels of corn. Can you not see what an incredible return on our investment this is? But we just have to be patient."

He might have continued, "With that kind of a return, we can eat all winter, feed the hogs, the cows, the mules, the chickens. We could even help Old Man Sam down the road who's been too sick to farm all year. And Miss Annie who lost her husband, John, back in February.

Remember when she cooked for us a few years back when you weren't feeling so well?"

I think you get the point.

To my knowledge, my grandmother never asked my grandfather to abandon the field. But to that man who felt compelled to walk away from McDonald's to save his family, I could relate.

My lovely wife had married an art teacher and had bought into that picture of her life, but things had changed drastically. I was a long way from the classroom now, working nights and weekends on my sign business and at Coca-Cola. On top of that, I was opening a McDonald's restaurant. For what I thought was an exciting, exhilarating journey, she was less than thrilled. My long nights working and studying seemed, to her, without an end in sight, and she would often say that it was taking too long and ask me, "Why don't you just stop?"

It was like being on a rollercoaster. Some people love the thrill of the looping, swooping ride. They throw their arms up and enjoy the moment. Other people, however, don't find it amusing at all. They don't like the feeling of their heart racing or the experience of having their breath taken away. That was my wife. She hated the ride she was on and eventually would want off, but I loved her, and I wanted her to stay.

I knew that behind all of her reservations was fear. She saw me moving in a different direction and it was outside of her, and in fact both of our, comfort zones. But I also knew that the desire for comfort could kill your purpose. I was on a path that was not just about me, or even her. How often does a black man have the opportunity to be the first to do something of that magnitude in Birmingham, Alabama? I had to make tough decisions, not for my comfort, but for the good of the greater community, I thought. I knew the ministry aspect of getting this restaurant. I knew what it would mean to the Birmingham community for a black man to own a major franchise business: the jobs and the relationships it might provide, the symbol of hope it could represent.

I did the best I could to prolong our time together, but I knew as my completion date for training with McDonald's was nearing the end, so was my wife's patience for this new normal that was becoming our lives.

To my daughter, I would say: What good are your successes if we don't remember our community or forget how much our community has done for us?

To my cousin, I would say: Focus on the good and the pleasant in the midst of unpleasant situations.

16

FIGHT FOR WHAT IS YOURS

By 1988, I reached a point in my training where an on-site tenure at Hamburger University was required. But by then I had used up all of my vacation time with Coca-Cola. It seemed like I had come to a fork in the road. I went to my boss, Brent, at Coca-Cola to discuss my impending choice with him.

"To complete this exercise with McDonald's," I explained to Brent, "I have to do a two-week finale in Oakbrook, Illinois. I only have one week of vacation left. I am at the end, I'm afraid. I just don't have any more time."

"Larry, you are going at this pretty hard," Brent replied. "You take a week off and I want you to spend it with your family. When you finish that, go ahead and take those two weeks for Hamburger University."

I was stunned by Brent's generosity. But there was a lesson to learn from it. When you do a good job for your employer, it is an investment not only for your boss and his company, but in yourself. I had built up enough equity in Coca-Cola to merit this offer. Perhaps many years of consecutive perfect attendance was paying off in a way I had never even imagined as I faithfully clocked in, day in and day out. And maybe all of those Saturdays and Sundays were being recognized as well.

As I have said before: *Work for life, and watch life work for you.*

And, as I shared in an earlier chapter, rules are generally made for the lowest common denominator—for the employees who would otherwise come in late or leave early, who would otherwise use company cars for personal benefit, or who would take more vacation time than they deserve, need, or have earned. But whether for the lowest common denominator or not, they must be respected. So do not misread me and think that I am suggesting that you can unilaterally decide when rules apply to you or not. You are not entitled to make that decision!

The key is, I think, to put in the hours and the efforts to convince the rulemakers that they do not have to denominate you among the lowest and regulate you accordingly. Get the rulemakers to a place where they look at you instead as among the highest multipliers. If you are recognized as being in the latter category, any company worth its salt will, whether out of appreciation or self-interest or both, treat you accordingly. You will leave the rules made for the lowest common denominators for those poor souls. Let them, with their selfish ways, bargain with Life for the proverbial penny. They will find that Life will pay them no more than that.

I, on the other hand, had bargained for more. So, with Robert's and Coca-Cola's blessing, I headed off to Illinois and Hamburger University. The vision of owning my own store was coming into view and, two weeks later, with my "on-campus" residency in Oakbrook completed, I could look back proudly on having completed the McDonald's training, not in the nearly two-year projection, but in one year and one week. During that time, I made the Dean's List and earned top honors, including the prestigious Gold Hat Award, the top honor bestowed at Hamburger University.

At this point, after excelling in the McDonald's training program, I was, of course, enthusiastically anticipating being approved for my first franchise store. After all, my hard work over the last year and a half was focused on that culminating moment when I could walk into my very own McDonald's restaurant. Not only was that moment going to change the trajectory of my life, but the lives of my family and those in the surrounding community. I was so excited, I could taste it.

My journey to that first store, however, was not quite finished. I had one more unanticipated and, in the end, hard-fought battle to fight. One more challenge stood between me and my dream of owning my own business—and since it took the form of the largest McDonald's franchise owner in the Southeast, the challenge was considerable.

At the time, the franchisee in question possessed hard-earned territorial rights to Birmingham (and beyond). That meant that any restaurant that McDonald's chose to open in his particular geographic area automatically belonged to him. Fortunately, that territorial agreement was coming to a close just as I was completing my training exercise. I thought that the expiration of the agreement was, as far as all parties would be concerned, opening a clear path for a new owner such as myself to move into the market. I even thought that the existing franchisee would be excited to welcome the first African American owner in Birmingham into the fold. After all, I had excelled at Hamburger University and the two of us shared former careers in advertising. We had much in common, I thought, and so I called him to seek his advice and counsel.

To my surprise, my first call elicited no response. I called him again. No response. And again. Again, no response. By now, I was beginning to wonder if the landed franchisee was, despite my earlier hopes to the contrary, less than excited about a new McDonald's restaurant opening within two miles of his home office—and being owned by an African American at that.

It was, to say the least, a disappointing turn of events. I came to suspect that his stonewalling was an indication that he was going to do everything he could to make certain that my attempt to enter into the McDonald's Birmingham family of owners would be met with a closed door. What he did not know, however, was that I was used to encountering closed doors. And, furthermore, I was both motivated and capable of fashioning my own key.

Sadly, it all felt very familiar. It was like being back at Goodwyn Junior High or the early days working in the Coca-Cola sign shop. The year was 1991 but, once again I was reminded that while the rest of the world might be rapidly embracing a global economy with all of the inherent challenges and considerations of a diverse world population, there were still people who were preoccupied with questions of who was black and who was white. What a small, narrow-minded, insignificant, and trivial mindset. After all, more than ninety percent of the world's population is neither black nor white.

Fortunately for me, I was no longer a wide-eyed twelve-year-old, frightened and unversed in the challenges ahead. Instead, I was a seasoned adult, ready to take on a world that was pretending it was not ready for me. I girded myself for a challenge and took matters into my own hands.

With a few circumspect phone calls and inquiries, I identified a date in which my quarry would be in his office all day. I then cleared my schedule so that I could take as long as necessary to visit with him and, steeling myself for what might be a long day and a difficult conversation, presented myself at the franchisee's office.

When I arrived, his assistant asked if I had an appointment. I told her that I did not, but that I was there simply to personally thank him for all that he had done in support of my development. Perplexed, the woman delivered my message, only to return to tell me that the man could not come out to meet me.

"That's fine," I told her. "I know he must be busy. I'll just wait until he has a free moment."

With that said, I settled into my seat in his waiting room and proceeded to wait—for hours. He would not come out and I would not leave. I literally held him hostage in his own office.

Ultimately, he had no choice but to emerge. I suppose he had had plenty of time to develop a plan of attack, and when he unleashed it on me it was, sadly, what I had expected. He shared with me a number of locations at which I could operate a new restaurant—and, not surprisingly, none were in my hometown of Birmingham.

Not good enough, I told him. Birmingham was my home, and I wanted to own a store in my hometown. Furthermore, it was time for businessmen like me to shoulder my old nemesis, Jim Crow, to the sidelines—even in a city like Birmingham.

The franchisee, however, would not concede. To him, Birmingham was off limits, and, right or wrong, he forced an impasse. For several weeks after that meeting, I made no progress in my efforts to secure a franchise of my own in Birmingham.

Fortunately, I had been selected to be a member of the 1990 class for Leadership Birmingham, where I had had the good fortune to make the acquaintance of attorney Rod Maxx. When I shared my frustrations with Rod, he quickly offered to intercede. I should add that he just as quickly refused to accept any payment for his time and effort. Rod recognized an injustice and, for him, rectifying that injustice seemed compensation enough.

To that end, Rod requested a meeting with the McDonald's regional manager. To our disappointment, he only offered us the "courtesy" of an interview in his car as he traveled about town on business. We were, seemingly, worth little more than that.

Candidly, I was embarrassed and even angered by such treatment. But I reminded myself that *if I can't take anything, I can't have anything.* And this time I had a lawyer by my side. Suffice it to say that my lawyer friend shared a few select but choice words with the regional manager on our ride around Birmingham. Those words were bereft of legal jargon but, whether despite that or because of it, they cut right to the heart of the matter. A letter to the regional manager soon followed; it further explained and emphasized our disappointment at the situation at hand.

It took some three months, but McDonald's finally offered the Heritage Towne Center location to me, tucked into Birmingham's historic Titusville community. I suspect that somewhere up the chain of command at McDonald's, our letter reached someone who was no fonder of old Jim Crow than I was. Whoever that person was, I owe him or her, and the McDonald's corporation, a debt of gratitude for doing the right thing. As an African American entrepreneur, I was now positioned to open a McDonald's in a community that had provided homes to the solid backbone of Birmingham's African American middle class, a scant mile from where future Secretary of State Condoleezza Rice's father had preached at Westminster Presbyterian Church.

For a time, however, it looked like the securing of McDonald's approval was the easy part—even as the dust settled, I still needed to come up with $164,000 to actually own the restaurant. But I did, and my store's grand opening finally arrived in July 1992.

As we threw open the restaurant's doors that morning, I was on top of the world. Everything was in place, my staff was flashing their bright McDonald's smiles, and my family and friends all came out to support me. So did Claude Nielsen, the president of Coca-Cola Bottling United. It was his business acumen I had admired so much over the years. It was enough of an event that we had local politicians in line to buy Egg McMuffins and sausage biscuits while local news crews covered the event. This was my public victory dance for all of the hard work I had invested in my dream to be my own boss.

But then, right in the midst of my celebration, the Birmingham franchisee and his business partner arrived on the scene. Barely acknowledging me, they strolled casually into the restaurant and then, unbelievably, the franchisee sauntered behind the counter—*my* counter. Meanwhile, his business partner sidled up to me

"You know you can't run a McDonald's, don't you?" he challenged.

Stunned by the sheer rudeness of what was unfolding, I could not even muster a response. He slowly surveyed the scene and then continued. "Yeah, we will own this in six months," he sneered.

For a moment, my knees weakened. Clearly they were watching and waiting for me to fail. But the moment passed and, in the place of the doubt that had momentarily festered, I found a new resolve. Their lack of confidence in my success, I decided, would provide even more of the incentive I needed to win the battle that had clearly been joined. I only wish that I had had, at that particular moment, the presence of mind to have passed him a thank-you note on his way out for the inadvertent motivation that they had provided me to push beyond what I had ever thought imaginable.

Some two months later, the franchisee and his minion returned to my store, this time with an offer to buy out my business. Again, they warned me that my restaurant was doomed to fail and that the smart thing would be for me to to beat a hasty retreat.

In response to their insulting challenge, I redoubled my efforts to succeed. I worked to make my location a beacon for the Titusville community. To its residents and my other guests, we offered signature service with unparalleled leadership and professionalism, as I made a point of greeting every customer with kindness and respect on each visit.

Another two to three months passed. My rival franchisee came to visit again. Again, he made the same offer. Again, I simply renewed my efforts to succeed. Over the course of my first year in business, this scenario played out three times. In the end, I took great comfort in remembering the Biblical prophecy found in the story of David. "Your enemies will become your footstool," the story said, and before the decade was out, I not only had succeeded with my first store but had bought two of my rival's McDonald's.

David, it seemed, had defeated Goliath once again.

But that wasn't the end of David's relationship with Goliath. After it became clear that I was not going to "bow out" or "sell out" of the McDonald's business, we eventually grew into a working relationship that was both personal and professional. Together we made significant contributions to our local and national McDonald's marketing efforts by combining the collective experiences that we both brought from our previous lives . . . and we did just that on a myriad of marketing/advertising projects.

As it turns out, the franchisee was a pretty big name on Broadway. Two of his productions even earned Tony Awards. Quite often, he would set me up for the best seats in the house when I had occasion to take in a musical in New York. And I was one of the last individuals to meet with him in his office—a private meeting that he insisted on having with me just three weeks before he passed away at ninety-nine years of age. Ninety-nine years old . . . and just as full of passion at that meeting as he was the day I met him in the late 1980s. As I think about our relationship, I think that we might all be amazed if we could know the real value of what it truly means to work together. I am just glad that, in the end, he and I had that opportunity. I came to appreciate him for his passion, his creative talents, and his philanthropy. He was, for example, instrumental in starting Ronald McDonald House Charities in Alabama. And I like to think that he came to appreciate those similar traits in me.

When your purpose is to render service to your community by breaking barriers, especially of a racial kind, the path is going to be a thorny one. The things you experience along the way are usually those that cannot easily be endured by the average person. But aren't we all, for the most part, average people? Nevertheless, we all have within us the inherent ability to function and perform at above-average levels. We just need to give ourselves permission to do so.

The humiliation and intimidation I endured at the hands of the embittered franchisee in the early days of our relationship would have made many people throw in the towel. But as I told myself, that man's actions and attitudes did not define *me*—rather, they defined *him* and *his* character. If I didn't internalize his actions, then they would have no power over me. My self-confidence and my work ethic would be a shield that protected me from any foolishness that tried to penetrate my heart or mind.

One of my fellow operator friends, George, told me how he considered joining Dr. Martin Luther King Jr. and the protestors during their 1960s civil rights campaign. He agreed to go through the training to prepare to face the counter-protesters, hecklers, and even abusive authorities in the marches and demonstrations for civil rights. The organizers began the training session by emphasizing to George and the others that no matter what was done to them, they had to keep marching. Then the training leaders went down a list of things that could possibly happen.

"They might hit you," they told George and the others. George just nodded.

"They might throw things at you. They might kick you."

George continued to sit there.

"They might spit on you."

At that point, George stood up from his chair, pulled out of his pocket the little cash he had, handed it to the group leader, and wished them well.

"I wanted to march for freedom," George told me, "but if someone dared to spit on me, it was going to be another story."

George knew he wasn't built for such possibilities, nor was he willing to prepare himself for such an experience. I suppose I admired—and still admire—his acute sense of self-awareness, as well as having the courage to say "this isn't for me."

I know what George would have been facing, and it would not have been an easy road to walk. I have been called "nigger," "boy," and "coon" by ignorant, ill-informed white folks, just about as much as I have been called "Oreo" and "Uncle Tom" by ignorant, ill-informed black folks. But somewhere along the line, I decided that I would manage to bear it all. I knew there was much more at stake than ego. And so I kept going—and keep going—because I believe that what I am doing is not so much for me as it is for my immediate and extended family and for my current and extended community. Perhaps that's why, to this very day, I consider the battles I faced worth it all.

> To my niece, I would say several things:
>
> One, some of the most incredible and amazing achievements were forged by people who didn't have sense enough to know that they couldn't achieve them.
>
> Two, be patient in your pace of progression. Be steady, methodical, and thorough. Take one step at a time. Anyone who runs up to a ladder with intentions of jumping to the tenth rung will end up back on the ground . . . again!
>
> Finally, with respect to your detractors, to those who would wish you harm, and to those that would revel in your rapid demise, find a way to love and appreciate them, for they will make you strong. You will come to credit them for much of your strength, courage, and resilience.

17

CLIMB YOUR MOUNTAIN

Some moments in life you never forget. They are seared into your memory because the weight of the experience is so great. You remember what you were wearing, what time of day it was, and you even recall the weather.

One such moment, from more than twenty-five years ago, comes to mind. It was a gorgeous, sunny day, sometime around 10 o'clock in the morning. I was on the second floor of the headquarters of First Commercial Bank. I had on my bluest blue suit and a starched white shirt. It was an appropriate uniform for the occasion, I thought. But the beauty of the day and the meticulousness of my clothing were a stark contrast to the turmoil and uneasiness that was bubbling inside me. I was afraid.

Before me stretched the largest table I had ever seen in my life—especially one that you did not eat from! Two life-size, hand-painted portraits of the bank's founders hung on the room's wall. One of those portraits was of Richard Anthony, who had extended me the offer to be here today. Around that table sat a dozen of the wealthiest men in Birmingham. They were the men who had asked me, a scant year after I had opened my first McDonald's, to serve on the bank's board of directors. I would be the first African American ever to do so. In the midst of that very remarkable moment, one thought reverberated in my head—I was now on the board of a bank, and my mother never even had a checking account!

As I marveled over that irony, the secretary passed out our binders.

Our names were embossed on the fronts of each of the red binders. I ran my fingers across the letters of my name and then slyly looked around the room to see if my book was just as red as the other members'. It was—and, for me, that made the moment real.

The variances between the worlds sitting at that table were startling. Most men there represented a second or third generation of seasoned business success. As children, many had attended prestigious boarding schools, with spring breaks on distant islands and Christmas vacations spent skiing in the Rockies. Their children would enjoy the same.

I, on the other hand, hailed from Montgomery's Madison Park neighborhood, a proud but humble community established by a collection of former slaves. My childhood and adolescence had been little more than the precursors to my ultimate fight to be recognized as a full-fledged man. It was a contest fought in a world where so many had questioned and resisted that status as such simply because of the color of my skin. Now I was at the starting line of a journey into this very foreign world and, looking around the conference room table, I knew that everyone else already had a head start. I felt that I didn't belong at that table. I was ill-equipped and ill-prepared. Even worse, I felt that everyone in that room knew it.

But as the minutes ticked by and I settled into my seat, I planted my feet on the floor and tried to allow myself to embrace my new role. Being at that table was daunting, but it was a mountaintop experience. I had worked so hard to get to that moment. Not only was I now a member of this elite fraternity of businessmen, but, as I reminded myself, I had also just opened the first black-owned McDonald's franchise in Birmingham.

Yes, I was on a mountaintop.

In fact, probably not coincidentally, that moment in that boardroom drew my thoughts to one of my favorite illustrations that I like to sketch when I make my growth and development argument to anyone who will listen. I draw it this way.

Off in the far left corner of a stark white sheet of drawing paper (see next page) stands a man at the foot of a mountain that seems to reach all the way to the heavens. He's tiny in comparison. This man has never climbed a mountain before and doesn't have the appropriate tools or equipment. He's not properly dressed, and he even seems to be wearing tennis shoes. But regardless of what he doesn't have, he has the heart to take a first step.

He takes that first step and begins climbing the mountain. As he ascends, the man discovers some tools—a rope, a pick, and maybe a flashlight. He takes advantage of them . . . and that helps him climb a little higher. Along the way, he might acquire the right shoes, discarded by a previous climber, maybe even with some crampons for the icy patches ahead. He's able to go a little faster and even higher.

As he rises even higher, a few people are waiting to share their rations with him. You see, they too are impressed with his heart for mountain climbing. Being seasoned climbers, they naturally appreciate such spirit. They could have viewed me as an interloper on "their" mountain, or laughed at or ridiculed me. But they did not. Quite the contrary. Instead, each member of that party of experienced climbers—just as every person sitting at that boardroom table had done for me—cheers the novice climber on. They even throw ropes down to him to help him out of particularly tight spots—just like those board members had done for me.

Such support sustains the climber. He climbs higher. Often, the weather is brutal, the terrain is rough, and the man is tempted to turn around—but he doesn't. He is determined to keep going. Somewhere along that climb, he asks, and answers, that question I formulated earlier: Why not win?

Then, before he knows it, this man has done an amazing thing, something no one he knows has ever done—he has climbed a MOUNTAIN. He stands on the summit and embraces the vista before him. It's filled with beauty. And to think, he started out with only a pair of tennis shoes and a goal.

There are people who have the fanciest mountain climbing gear that money can buy, but they never get past the foot of a mountain because they won't take that first step. I didn't want it to ever be said that I didn't take the steps I needed to climb my mountain of life. So, throughout the years, I have worked long hours, read numerous books, endured racial attacks, lost sleep, and even lost friends. It was grueling, and sometimes lonely, even with the support of people along the way. But I can look around and see that I have climbed a mountain.

My presence at that table on that day—and my continued presence on that same board twenty-four years later—set into motion what I hoped would be the start of second and third generations of Thorntons sitting at that same table—or tables like it. If I, an awkward, poor kid from Madison Park, with an art degree rather than an MBA, could become an entrepreneur who earned his place on the boards of major institutions, what could my son, my niece, my cousin, and my grandchildren accomplish? The sky's the limit for them and all of us. I plan on doing my very best to make sure they know that, even though entrepreneurship is something new for my family, just as it is for many people in my community. If it takes a shift inside of the DNA of those with my last name or those within my community, I'll keep working at it.

Changing the trajectory of a generation is no easy feat, and being the first and sometimes only African American in a lot of situations can be a lonely place. Nevertheless, I grit my teeth, straighten my back, and walk a journey that I hope will create a path for my family. Everything I have done, and continue to do, is because in my mind's eye I see faces: ones of those who have passed on, ones who greet me daily, and ones who have yet to be born.

Because my experiences, along with my approach to them, have allowed me to enjoy morsels of fruit from so many trees that I took no part in planting, pruning, or picking, today I want to plant a few trees of my own, in an effort to quench the hunger and thirst of others—both within my community and beyond it. And if those trees provide cool shade or nourishing fruit to a trailblazing mountaineer, so much the better!

To my niece, I would say: You may not have the right background, or education, or equipment, or even the right shoes, but do not let that deter you. Serendipity is real. Trust in it. Remember that your good luck will come in proportion to your hard work. So go find your mountain and start climbing. The harder you climb, the better the view will be.

18

NEW PEAKS AND NEW VALLEYS

There was only one problem with my mountaineering sketch—it showed a solitary climber. My wife was nowhere in the image. And I'm afraid that was not merely an oversight.

When I excitedly told my wife about the invitation to join First Commercial's board, she just sighed.

"There you go again," she said.

At this point, things seemed to be happening at a rapid-fire pace for me. I was harvesting the fruit of having changed my thinking and having positioning myself to work for Life. Life was rewarding me. It was an amazing feeling. A former sign painter was now consulting for Birmingham Coca-Cola, owning his own McDonald's restaurant, and serving on the board of directors at First Commercial Bank. That was pretty damn good for a kid from Madison Park. Nevertheless, I suppose her reaction was not completely unexpected. She was already unhappy with the demands Coca-Cola and my new restaurant were putting on me, as well as the uncertainty and stress they had injected into our lives. She felt—rightly, I admit—that service on the bank board would be one more thing to keep me busy.

I tried to get her to see the importance of it all. "Look at the message this would send to the black and white communities," I said. "Look at what this will do for black people."

She was not impressed.

Her reaction hammered home an important lesson to me: different people bring different perspectives to the same situation. It reminds me of how a giraffe and an ant can look at the exact same thing, but, because the giraffe's view is from high above and the ant's is from down below, their perspectives are completely different. They could both be looking at the same molehill, but one would see a mountain and the other would see a speck of dirt.

The core of any disagreement can quite often be reduced to a difference in perspective. Your goals or objectives may be based on something that is ten years down the road. The other person's goals or objectives, however, may be based on the here and now. It is not that anyone is more right or wrong; it's just different. And, unless you can find a common ground, that difference can be fatal to a relationship.

Ultimately, despite tears shed and prayers said by both of us, my wife and I realized that we would not be able to continue our life journey together. She had married a schoolteacher and, perhaps understandably, she had expected me to be a schoolteacher for life. But at this point, I was far from the classroom and distancing myself even further each day. She was a beautiful and virtuous woman, but the stress of seeing her life careening off in an unexpected direction, and seemingly picking up speed, was too much for her to bear. I never wanted to write a sentence like this in my life story but in 1994 we divorced. Together, we agreed that I would have custody of our ten-year-old son.

They say that the ancient Chinese had a curse: "May you live in interesting times." Well, my life had certainly become interesting. There I was, owning my first McDonald's restaurant, consulting for Coca-Cola, serving on the board of directors of a bank, and now solely responsible for homework, doctors' and dental appointments, and PTA meetings. But *if you can't take anything, you can't have anything.* The more you can take, the more you can have.

As heartbreaking as this turn of events was, I chose to press forward. And when I reflect today on the millions of dollars I have been able to generate within my community, the thousands of jobs my restaurants have provided, and the legacy of business ownership, I can say that the rewards were worth the wounds.

Of course, it was all easier said than done. Some might make the mistake of looking at me (particularly if they have not read this book!) and thinking, "Wow, I would like to be doing what Larry is doing." It is easy to say that, isn't it? It is far less easy to do it. Unfortunately, we see so many examples of wishing and saying rather than investing and doing—even in our own families. And even in the warmth of a family gathering, the ugly truth too often reveals itself: "I want to do what you do, but I am not willing to do what you did."

To my uncle, I would say: It is not as much about the "doing" as much as it is about the "did." The "did" is where the value is. Be willing to withstand the heat of the fire. Bear the winds and rains of the storms, then rest in the assurance that the impending blue skies and sunshine will take care of themselves.

19

WORK YOUR FIELD

When it comes to business—and life—nature is an excellent teacher. I never have to look too far from the lessons learned from watching and assisting my daddy and granddaddy while they worked in the fields. Just as there was plenty of corn and peas during harvest time, the seeds of wisdom were likewise bountiful.

It is just my humble opinion, but the parable of the sower is really a story about economics. In that tale, you have a person who works night and day in the field sowing seeds and doing everything he can to protect his crop with no immediate reward. While he works, not only do the elements bear down upon him, but so do constant distractions and detractors. The sower is often faced with the choice of staying in the field and continuing to work, or leaving his post due to the discomforts that might confront him.

When you really think about it, the sower is you and me. And the field is life. When we have a purpose that has placed us "in the field" to sow, we simply cannot allow the heat, the birds, the rocks, and the thorns of life to drive us out. We have to stay in the field and stay the course of building our business or accomplishing our dream. And, just as in the cycle of sowing and reaping, immediate rewards are often rare in business. The payoff comes from consistently putting in the work. But if we put in the time and the work, efforts exerted on well-tended ground will more likely than not lead to a bountiful harvest beyond our wildest imaginings.

Find Your Field

When you look at a farmer's field, you have to be able to see not what it is but what it can become and what it can yield. Some people scan the field and just see that it will yield work. They are the ones who walk away.

Others, however, see the potential. Sure, they see the work that awaits, but they also see the prospect of a fall harvest. Those are the ones who stay—and prosper.

I heard a story about a shoe salesman who was sent to a Third World country to try to acquire some business. When he arrived, he saw that everyone in the area was barefoot. He promptly called the home office. "This is a waste of time," he told his boss. "No one here wears shoes."

So he got back on the plane and returned home.

But on the next flight into that Third World nation, there was another shoe salesman. He also saw the city of shoeless people. And, like the first salesman, he also called his boss. But he called home with far more excitement in his voice.

"Boss, we're going to make a fortune. No one here has shoes!"

One man saw the obstacle, the other saw the potential.

It's Lonely in the Field

I've often wondered (perhaps most of us have) why, in the whole farming scheme, we couldn't simply start with the good ground. Why couldn't rich, fertile soil, soft and tilled, come first in the process? If one's introduction to farming occurs during the harvest season . . . why, this farming thing can appear rather attractive. But farming is more about the *did* than the *doing*. What *did* the farmer do? Did he spend the long hours turning the ground in April and May and planting the seed, and then, in the sweaty summer, was he out there fighting the bugs and chopping the weeds? If he *did*, then he can hope to reap a bountiful harvest. If not, then not.

If you are trying to create a business or reach a major goal, expect a lonely journey. Few people will join you out in your field. When others are relaxing or watching TV, you will be in the field. When it is hot and the bugs are swarming, you will be in the field. In the field, pressures and responsibilities will weigh heavily on you, and few people will be enticed to shoulder the burdens alongside you. You may find some help along the way—remember my mountaintop drawing—but days are lonely in the field (and, for that matter, climbing a mountain). You will go to the field early and come home late. You'll leave some people behind as you go to the field, and, by the time you come home, some people will not have waited for you.

Even when you bring in your harvest, you will still be lonely in your intimate knowledge of just what that bounty required. People will see your harvest, but they will not know the pain you endured when you were laying down the seed, hacking at the weeds, or picking the produce. Faced with the bounty of a harvest, many will assume it came easily. They will take it for granted.

Don't let the inevitable loneliness of the field deter you. You cannot reap the rewards unless you put in the service. You have to stay the course and know that eventually a harvest will come.

Rid Yourself of the Weeds

My granddaddy also understood that after you have devoted your time to personally digging holes, carefully planting each seed, and making sure that they are watered and fed, weeds will spring up and attempt to choke the life out of your growing plants. That was how it was with my granddaddy's crops.

The field of life, in which you plant your seeds of business, has its own weeds. Those weeds can take on several forms. Maybe they are employees, or members of your staff, or, most unfortunately, members of your own family. In the same way that my granddaddy was the guardian of his seeds' output, you have to be the guardian of your business, for that business represents your seeds. And that means that in the field of life, you may have to root out the weeds that seek to take the nutrients meant to nurture your seeds.

That can be a very difficult thing when the weed has your same surname. Although I have not had any formal business training, I have stumbled upon one fact of business that I know to be consistently true: the business will always dictate to you exactly what needs to happen to ensure its sustenance. When you understand that, you will understand that it is up to you as the business owner to act decisively, minus any intruding emotions, and without respect to circumstance or person.

Sadly, I speak from experience. As the years passed with McDonald's, I listened to my business and it told me that I needed to terminate my own daughter. In many ways, my daughter was a natural for the business—quick-witted, great with the crew and customers, and had excelled in her work at Hamburger University. Frankly, she was naturally and inherently sharper than either my son or me. But she had always been somewhat passive about the whole McDonald's experience. She lacked the passion, the discipline, and the interest that, in a business like ours, separates success from failure.

"Daddy, I really don't like this MacDonald's stuff," my daughter would often say to me.

After hearing that complaint one time too many, I drew upon my artistic creativity and responded as best I could.

"You remind me of a shipwrecked people on a distant and deserted island," I said to her. "They've been relegated to this godforsaken island, generation after generation for more than four hundred years, with little to no hope of ever being rescued." I did not tell her that my choice of four hundred years was not accidental—the transatlantic slave trade had endured for four centuries.

"But one morning at sunrise, they noticed something strange on the distant horizon," I continued. "It was a most unusual sight. As the object moved closer, they realized that it was a ship—a ship large enough to rescue everyone on the island. Practically everyone on the island was overwhelmed with joy. The day of deliverance for them, and their families, and their future offspring, was at hand. But a small group of islanders did not see it that way. They stood resolutely alone on a remote part of their island and, rather than embrace this opportunity, complained to one another, 'I don't like that ship . . . why did they paint it that color?"

In short, I tried to appeal to her emotional side as to what it would mean to our community to have a young black woman to represent ownership of a McDonald's franchise. It would send an irrefutable and unspoken message to black females throughout the South. But nothing seemed to resonate.

Then came a three-day evaluation by the McDonald's regional office that revealed failing QSC (quality, service, cleanliness) grades in her restaurant. The fact that her restaurant failed miserably was not necessarily the biggest problem; the bigger issue was her passive and apathetic approach to the failure.

It was obvious that the business was speaking to me loudly and clearly with information that I did not want to receive. How could it have come to this? The irony was particularly painful in that providing a legacy for my children was, after all, one of the purposes for my going into business in the first place. But I had to move on this issue—and move decisively.

I separated my beloved daughter from my business and, as difficult as it was, I know that my business has, through the gift of twenty-five years of success, thanked me for having the courage to make that decision.

Birds Will Come for the Seed

One thing you can be sure of is that, after you have planted your field, rapacious birds will come for some of your seed. For some folks, that is a hard pill to swallow, but you have to accept it. It is an inherent reality of life.

In 1994, a gunman robbed my store. After all of the time, effort and sacrifice that I had invested in my store, I wanted to do everything I could to find the culprit. When my employees told me that they knew who the robber was and where he lived, it fueled my urge to bring this thief to justice.

But what would happen if I left my store to get a gun and go after that criminal? What if you were to get a gun and chase the birds from your field? At that point, as Jim Rohn stated so simply, you have now left the field. No, you have to stay in the field and continue to sow, weed, and reap. You can't be in the business of chasing birds. That's what the police are for. If you don't have the self-discipline to stay at work in your field, you will end up spending more time chasing birds.

Yes, birds will steal some of your seed—and you have to be okay with that reality. Our job is to sow, ignore the birds, push past the rocks, endure the thorns, and enjoy the eventual good ground. We will most certainly get distracted, but we cannot let ourselves be sidelined.

Don't Fall for Fakers

Another thing I learned in the field is that there will be times when you think you have something authentic when, in actuality, it is not. My daddy had a half-acre garden and would often plant corn. Now, before corn fully manifests into the ears that we all know, it looks in its infancy stage very similar to Johnson grass—small, floppy, narrow and green. As a young kid, I had spent enough days in the field with my daddy and his corn that I thought I knew exactly what corn looks like.

One day, I questioned my dad as to why he was chopping away at what I thought was corn. To my eyes, the infant stalks of "corn" were dispersed generously and fortuitously about the rows of the garden.

"Boy, that ain't no corn," he chuckled. "That's Johnson grass."

Of course, I wasn't convinced. How could something that looked almost identical to corn . . . not be corn? So I found an area of the garden with a good supply of what I discerned to be corn and set about cultivating it. I fertilized it with manure and chopped away the other weeds from my corn.

It was going to be my way of proving to Dad that my corn was going to grow into just as much of a cornstalk as his.

The end of the summer brought the final judgment on our disagreement. Dad reaped ears of corn from his rows. And I simply had some strong, shiny, and good-looking Johnson grass.

I would relive that moment with my own child some years later when my oldest daughter brought her first boyfriend home. She was convinced that she had corn. From her perspective, he dressed like corn, talked like corn, walked like corn . . . But because of my many years of having to differentiate between corn and Johnson grass, I saw, with just a few lines of verbal exchange, that my daughter was dealing with Johnson grass. My daughter argued up and down with me that I was wrong. She was adamant, but so was I. My years of being in the presence of Johnson grass had given me a careful eye for what was real and what was fake. When all was said and done, my daughter's guy was, in fact, a big patch of Johnson grass. And eventually she also saw it.

Unfortunately, for some people, the truth is never clear. They will spend the better part of their lives nurturing and caring for Johnson grass. Through many tears, heartaches, and pain, they will labor feverishly to do the impossible—to change Johnson grass into corn.

What Do You Do with the Harvest?

Once you have sown the seed, protected the harvest, and watched it grow, what's next? A good sower will not only produce enough for him and his family but more than that. You will likely face such surpluses as well. So, what do you do with a harvest of thirty-, sixty-, or even a hundred-fold?

To me, the answer has always been simple. You go back and feed the farmers and the field hands. Again, what you are building is not just for you. Your harvest is for the community, too. "Community" is a four-syllable word until we can let go and make it into one syllable: "we."

What a great place to be—to have a bountiful harvest to share with your community. Simply put, those who are willing to stay in the field will be able to affect their lives and those of the people around them.

To my nephew, I say: Everything that we harvest comes from, by, and through the community. Our rewards are not meant solely for us. Such harvests are meant to be shared. What better place to share the fruits of our harvest than in the community that made it possible?

20

YOUR ULTIMATE SUCCESS
LIES IN THE SUCCESS OF OTHERS

Perhaps the surest measure of our success is the success of those around us. To be sure, there are moments when I feel so tall and so proud of what *I* have been able to accomplish. For those brief spells, I allow myself to stand in grateful awe of what I've been able to do. But I dwell there for only a moment.

It is dangerous to linger in that space for too long. For that reason, I intentionally step out of that place and allow myself to be drawn into an honest and genuine place of humility and gratitude. In that place, I am thankful for experiences both blissful and painful. I am thankful for individuals, positive or negative, that life seemed to deliberately and strategically place in my path. I am thankful for those experiences and individuals who afforded me opportunities to defy odds that seemingly gave me little hope of winning in life.

The funny thing about life is that oftentimes even experiences or individuals who, at first glance, seem outright horrific can, in the end, confer the greatest blessings. And although I hope it does not embarrass her for me to put her in this category, Pat Greensmith was one such person.

After I had logged four years in the restaurant business, McDonald's assigned Pat to me as a corporate business consultant. Like my old teacher Miss Nichols, Pat came to us with a definite agenda. Her agenda was, come hell or high water, to take my restaurants and everyone involved in them to a new level of operational awareness. She made no secret of her objective and was quite forthcoming with her tactics. I am not exaggerating when I say that her favorite catchphrase echoed in my dreams at two o'clock in the morning: "Any day. Any time. Any restaurant. I am subject to show up for an evaluation."

And indeed she did. After she showed up at my restaurants on two consecutive Sunday afternoons, I knew we were in for an interesting ride. As her assignment with me progressed, we had our share of disagreements and challenges but, happily, to both of our credits, we managed them tactfully and diplomatically. Before long, we had settled into an amenable approach to moving our business forward—although, as typical of Pat's style, I could never quite determine whose approach we actually implemented. In retrospect, assigning credit was unimportant. What mattered was that we advanced our operations platform to a new level—and that those levels are maintained today. Any way you look at it, the actual winner of our challenges and disagreements was the restaurant—and both Pat and I were more than satisfied with that.

Today, I thank Pat for being such a powerful catalyst in my business. I trace many of my personal milestones and accomplishments to her work with me. She found Tracey Twyman, my director of operations of more than eighteen years, for me. She was instrumental in my being asked to deliver a college commencement address for the first time. I even owe her a hallmark moment in my artistic career featuring Maya Angelou. We share a genuine friendship that will last a lifetime.

Oh, how grateful I am for other people. More and more, it seems that my mother's will became my will. Miss Nichols's confidence in me became my confidence in me. Claude Nielsen's and Richard Anthony's expectations of me became my expectations for myself. My son's pride for me became pride in myself. And Walker Jones's passion for what could be became my passion for what can be. How exceedingly grateful I am for other people!

Now how can a portion of my example be of service to someone else? We create better experiences for ourselves by facilitating better experiences for others. Did you ever think of it that way? Consider the Zig Ziglar quote: "You can have anything you want . . . as long as you help enough other people get what they want." That certainly does add merit to an inexplicable point: You will only be successful as long as enough other people want you to be. What a fantastic concept!

What if we felt it incumbent upon ourselves to seek opportunities to assist someone who is looking but does not yet see? Someone who is hearing but not listening. Someone who is strong but not exercising their strength? Someone who is able but is not maximizing their ability? Perhaps it is true that only what we do for others will last.

We're Not in This Alone

Lynda Hubka has, among other things, served as our administrative assistant and office manager for practically as long as I have been in business. She truly represents the heartbeat of our organization as well as the moral fiber and fortitude of our efforts. Entrusted with such reliance and faith, she is always on the watch for just the appropriate catchphrase, quote, or thought for the moment to share with me.

Once, Lynda was on a bank run when she called me to share an anonymous quote posted on the bank's drive-through window. It read: "BE KIND . . . for everyone you meet is involved in a great struggle."

"Wow!" I thought.

I put aside my work of the moment and began to dissect this power-packed quote. Not some of the people you meet but *everyone*. Not an occasional discomfort but a *great struggle*. Wow.

Somehow, just knowing that we're *all* dealing with grave challenges tends to bring a kind of placid calm to our own struggle. So be kind to others. And be kind to yourself.

Work Hard, Relate Hard

Sometimes a particular skill or procedural context drives the dictates and demands of a given business. Too often, I'm afraid, so much focus is placed on "doing things right" that we are negligent when it comes to "doing the right thing." Our restaurants are no exception.

To be a good restaurant manager, you have to master an understanding of the calibrations of our Coca-Cola fountain and shake/sundae units. An ice cream cone should weigh 2.5 ounces; a sundae, 5 ounces; a 16-ounce shake, 7 ounces. You should have an air-to-mix ratio of 40 percent on shakes and 55 percent on ice cream sundaes. To stay within acceptable product yield guidelines, the syrup-to-mix ratio for a shake is 1 ounce for every 7 seconds of shake drawn.

But if you *really* want to walk down the corridors of effective restaurant management, take five minutes on a Monday morning and ask the maintenance man/women how his/her weekend went and genuinely listen to the response. That is leadership.

To be a good restaurant manager, of course, you have to understand product weight, temperatures and holding times. If you are not getting 400–420 small orders of fries, weighing 2.5 ounces each; 264 medium fries weighing 4 ounces, and 174 large fries weighing 6 ounces from each 100 pounds of potatoes, then you are not going to make product-yield targets. This, in turn, will drive up food costs and reduce your restaurant's profitability. Every restaurant manager has to understand these ratios.

But if you *really* want to reside in the upper chambers of effective restaurant management, then spend five minutes in the crew room. Ask to see a photo of a baby or grandbaby. Ask how you can accommodate a crew's schedule for the next college semester. That is leadership.

To be a good restaurant manager, you should certainly know well the logistical steps of cash-handling procedures. Getting the cash into the registers, out of the registers, and into the safe, out of the safe, compiled into an accurate deposit, signed out on the deposit log, into the bank, and credited to the proper account are all paramount to the success of any quick service restaurant. Any manager who remains a manager has to be consistent in that process.

But if you really want to function at premium levels of significant restaurant management effectiveness, seek to master the timely employment of three little phrases we all learned in grade school: "*Thank you*," "*Please*," and "*Excuse me*." George Frazer, in his book *Success Runs in our Race*, refers to these three as the lubricants of life: *Thank you. Please. Excuse me.* They are absolutely necessary to deal with your superiors in business but are much more significant when interacting with your employees, associates, and subordinates. That is leadership.

Individuals who have invested in developing outstanding communications, human relations, and interpersonal skills have created an inestimable advantage for themselves. One of my most actionable examples of someone who has such strong people qualities is my colleague on the Coca-Cola Bottling Company United board of directors, Walker Jones. To observe Walker is to experience a composition of people talents, unified in a masterful symphony of success.

There is nothing like the overwhelming significance that one feels when greeted by Walker. I have witnessed her steadfast and consistent way of approaching people, whether conversing with some of our bottling line associates or our company's president and CEO. Everyone warrants a "please," a "thank you," or an "excuse me." Whether mingling at a thousand-dollar per head black-tie ticketed reception or championing a cause from a community center's folding chairs, Walker never forgets that she is interacting with individual human beings, each with his or her own sense of self-worth and identity. Throughout my private business career, I have taken advantage of opportunities to assess and improve my own people skills by way of Walker's unassuming example. She is a paragon for human relations and is certainly an advocate for the hopeful vision that all people matter, irrespective of their station in life, their job, or what you might perceive to be their usefulness to you at a particular moment.

> *To my niece, I would say: Corporations and/or organizations around the globe have little choice but to place high premiums on those persons who continuously strive to extend their reach in the areas of personal and people relations development. Other people can virtually lift us up and deliver us unto the desires of your heart. The reliable navigation of a certain course toward significant winning can only be achieved through and by other people.*

21

EMBRACE AN ATTITUDE OF GRATITUDE

Decades ago, on an otherwise unremarkable summer Saturday, and well before being on any corporate boards or owning my McDonald's restaurants, I realized something that fundamentally changed my outlook on life. "Realized" probably is not a strong enough word; rather, this new awareness hit me like a bolt out of the blue.

That particular Saturday afternoon, I was working just outside of my garage on what seemed to be my best design/graphic layout ever. It was for a good friend who was going into the shaved ice/snow cone business. The design was an open-face, custom-designed font with graduated colors of white, yellow, orange, and red, bordered with a two-inch jet-black outline on his white 8 x 14-foot concession trailer. It was looking good and coming together nicely. Then an unbidden thought stopped me cold.

At that moment, with a warm Alabama summer pushing the mercury in the thermometer toward the blue sky above, and a great piece of commercial art coming to fruition off to the side of a home that I owned and shared with my wife and family, a wave of gratefulness and gratitude crashed into me.

That feeling swaddled me tightly and put me in an incredible state of thankfulness—for my family, my job, my sign-painting skills, and even my good sense. For that moment, I was physically incapable of doing anything else but quietly reflecting on my life's unexpected blessings.

I thought back to Miss Nichols and how she had pulled me aside to speak words of encouragement even though she did not have to. I thought about being handpicked to be put in that tense situation at Goodwyn Middle School, which became a training ground for my future life. I thought of the pain and uncertainty of being terminated after four years of teaching, only to be hired at Coca-Cola, which gave me a chance to paint signs and learn about business.

Those were not the only gifts I counted in my head that day. Indeed, the more I thought, the more that list grew. As I tallied my list of blessings, I added to it the gratitude I felt for having affirmatively rejected the fate the customer at the Majik Mart had unknowingly tried to attach to me. You remember his mantra: "You and me ain't gonna never have shit in life. You know what I'm saying, bud?"

Well, I had become *someone* after all, and all I could do was be thankful and enjoy the fragrance of roses too plentiful to number. And, equally importantly, I knew that what I had achieved was not solely by the works of my own hands, but by a community of people, circumstances, and situations supporting me through all manner of challenges.

From that moment on, I felt selfish praying for mere things. That seemed so silly and frivolous in the grand scheme of things. And so I told myself that I was not going to ask for another thing for myself until I have expressed adequate gratitude for everything I had been given. Every day after that moment, more than thirty years ago, one word has been my guiding force: thankfulness. My thoughts are when we find ourselves kneeling, whether brought to our knees in prayer or forced to our knees by adversity, we ought to start with thanksgiving. My life, from then on, became transformed because I chose to live in a perpetual state of gratitude. I highly recommend it.

A part of being thankful is saying the words "thank you" to others. In the summer of 2015, I had an opportunity to visit with Attorney Solomon

Seay. You will recall that he was the crusading civil rights attorney who had set out to get black schoolchildren into previously all-white classrooms during the tumultuous 1960s. He had been the one to persuade my mother to sign me up for that integration project.

It might surprise you that in my youth I had no interest in thanking Attorney Seay for his role in my life. Rather, you could honestly say that I resented the man. At the time, I could not see how what he did was of benefit to anyone. It did not dawn on me that he was trying to help African Americans gain access to the freedoms that were rightfully ours. Nor could I see his own sacrifices. Even his own beloved daughter Sheryl was not spared from the process. She was also among the students thrust into the unwelcoming world of Goodwyn.

For many years afterwards, I did not see any of that. I saw only the pain and shame I experienced. For too long, I could not look past the discomfort of those days. I could not appreciate how the flame of that experience had forged the future Larry Thornton.

The passing of years, however, gave me the opportunity to reflect on the broader picture of my time at Goodwyn and why I was there. Looking at the whole picture, I could see the value and can appreciate the journey. Battle wounds and all, I am thankful—truly thankful—for that opportunity that ultimately positioned me to render a greater service to my community.

Blessed with that sense of perspective, I was therefore grateful when attorney Fred Gray set up a visit between Seay and myself. Like Seay, Gray was one of the African American lions of Alabama's civil rights bar members in the 1960. It seemed fitting that Gray had brokered this particular meeting.

The Solomon Seay I saw that day in 2015 was not, of course, the young attorney of the 1960s that I remembered, knocking on doors with a passion for social justice. Age had gripped him, and a sense of seasoned wisdom had replaced the fiery determination that once blazed in his eyes. But the passage of time had not diminished what Seay had accomplished for me and so many other African American children in Montgomery.

Sitting down next to Seay, I reminded him of my childhood friendship with his daughter, Sheryl, and our shared ninth-grade experiences at Goodwyn. I told him how, as a kid, I had been angry with him. And I shared with him that I now recognized that what he had done had helped to put me on a path of achievement—and for that I was grateful.

Seay seemed to appreciate my words, and I was glad to have had the opportunity to speak them. He died not long after our talk. "We won't find anyone to fill his shoes," one of his colleagues told the *Montgomery Advertiser* after his death. "We just hope we can find someone to walk in his tracks."

People like Solomon Seay were an inspiration. I remember as a child seeing very few doctors and lawyers in our community and thinking that they were special—almost anomalies, even—who must have been born to do this very unique work. The truth, however, was that there was nothing necessarily special about those fine people—or any of us for that matter. They were everyday common folks who had decided to do some very uncommon things.

Recognizing that truth gave me, an ordinary person, permission to aspire to do great things. I could do great things for myself, my family, and my community. And in the end, we would all be better for it.

To my grandson, I would say: Bathe regularly in the warm waters of gratitude; be grateful and express your gratitude often.

22

ENJOYING THE SHADE
PROVIDED BY OTHERS

As I reflect on my journey over the last twenty-five years, my mind goes to thoughts of a very special pecan tree down in Montgomery. That might sound silly, but there is a lesson there that I hope you won't miss.

When I was a little boy, my daddy planted that particular pecan tree. He found a wide open space, identified a perfect spot on the ground, and planted the sapling next to a stake to guide its growth. I loved pecans, so I was thrilled at the prospect of the mountain of nuts it would surely produce.

After a couple of years, the sapling grew into what I could recognize as a tree. But there were no pecans on this supposed pecan tree. Scratching my head, I searched out my daddy.

"Isn't this a pecan tree?" I asked him. "Where are the pecans?"

My daddy confirmed that it was indeed a pecan tree, but that it would be seven years before any pecans would be ready for me to eat, and ten years before there would be a full harvest.

Seven to ten years? That perplexed me. Why would anyone even bother to plant something that would not even manifest until nearly a decade later? It seemed like a waste of time. But my father was not planting that tree for himself. In fact, he died before enjoying the full harvest of it. He was planting a pecan tree so that I and many others in my family and community could enjoy its shade and fruit. And in that spirit, the tree was just as much for him as it was for us.

Daddy was thinking about me and not himself when he planned for that tree. He put it in a wide open field, and not next to the plum bushes, the peach tree, or the fig trees, so that its limbs could stretch out wide and provide lots of cool shade for anyone who wanted to sit underneath. He had thought of every detail, it seemed.

What my father did seems to be a theme in my life. I have been blessed to enjoy the fruit of harvests and the shade of trees that those who came before me planted. All that I am is a product of the sweat, tears, prayers, and lessons that so many people poured into me. And so I, in turn, have lived my life with the intent to plant trees and sow harvests so that many others can enjoy the benefits long after I am gone.

Today when I go to that piece of land down in Montgomery, the tree is still there. It is still producing bountiful pecans for all who want them. It is still providing shade to those who rest beneath its leafy branches. And when I see that tree, I cannot help but smile and think of my daddy, who never had the opportunity to see this tree in its fullness.

Faces on a Billboard

I remember visiting a school a few years ago and sharing lessons of this nature with the grade-school children who were crowded in the classroom to hear me speak. They were attentive and wide-eyed, hanging on my every word.

At the end of my talk, one little girl remarked, "Your picture should be on a billboard."

After enjoying a brief moment of pride, I realized that a teachable moment was before me. Gratefully, I leaned into it.

I told her that she was kind, but that if there were to be a billboard to honor me, I would first have to put my parents' pictures on it, for I would not be here without them and their sacrifices. I then told her that I would also have to put Miss Nichols's picture on there because her words made all the difference in putting me on the path I am on today. Then, I proceeded to list a number of individuals whose faces should be on that billboard before mine:

- Lynn Battle, who had the foresight of choosing the location of my first McDonald's—and convincing me, and helping me convince McDonald's, of such;
- Claude Nielsen, who spent countless hours teaching me to interpret a profit and loss statement;
- Chip Bivens, David Tony, and Hershell Hamilton, who taught me about the balance sheet;
- Richard Anthony, who invited me to serve on my first corporate board;
- A. G. Gaston, whose example motivated and encouraged me to do in my day what he did in his—to have my own business and to make it work;
- And my sister Barbara, who has been a constant support for all that I do and have done.

"You see," I told the little schoolgirl, "after putting up the faces of so many other deserving individuals, I don't imagine that there would be any room for mine."

The moral of the story is that we are here because a community of people helped us get here. We should not dare to stand in the sunlight and take all the praise for ourselves. The story might be about me, or at least might have me as a central character, but my accomplishments are not about me. It's about them.

Wall of New Beginnings

On the southern crest of Red Mountain, overlooking the city of Birmingham, stands a private dining and social club named The Club. Not just "t"he Club but "T"he Club. In fact, it is officially named The Club, Inc., and when the name is pronounced, the emphasis is on the "The." When it opened its doors in 1951, it quickly became the place where the city's business elite met to dine and dance. And, of course, as a Birmingham institution, its early days were circumscribed by the racism and segregation of the era. For many years, the only people with my skin color who walked the halls at The Club were the ones who were there to serve and clean.

Times have changed in Birmingham, however, and, not long ago, I became the first African American elected to The Club's board of governors. Then in 2016 I was elected to be the club's president—the only African American club president in the club's sixty-five-year history.

I was understandably proud of achieving that distinction. So were my nearly six thousand fellow club members. And that pride was reflected in the faces of the African Americans who worked at The Club. I knew my presence meant a lot to them, and I always found time to greet and speak with them. I did the same with The Club's white and Hispanic employees, males and females. I knew that my position was an indication of change in Birmingham, and positive change does not have to be a zero-sum game.

After my term as president ended, the general manager and the chef conspired to celebrate me with a feast that featured menu items from McDonald's transformed into gourmet dishes. Then, my 8 x 10 photograph was placed on the Past President's Wall. My smiling brown face was posted next to the faces of thirty-two white males. It was a rewarding moment, for too many reasons to recount or explain.

What would my mother, who said I had "special hands," think about my life now? What would my father, who taught me countless lessons and once said to me that I had a white man's job, think? What would Miss

Nichols, who saw me going to college even before I could see it myself, think? What would old Mr. Jim Crow and his followers say?

The fact that I can enjoy the fruit of many long nights, heartaches, and heartbreaks warms my heart, but it also fans the flame inside me to keep going. It fuels me to keep helping others so that one day more faces like mine—or like yours—will grace that same wall. In fact, I hope that they grace many others. As I put down my pen and bring this manuscript to a close, I hope that the experiences, lessons, and thoughts I've shared on these pages might help to make that happen.

You have a life to live. Why not win it?